Biblical Metaphors for the Holy Spirit

Book 1 of a trilogy about God the Holy Spirit

Michael E.J. Wright

malcolm down

PUBLISHING

First published 2023 by Malcolm Down Publishing Ltd.
www.malcolmdown.co.uk

27 26 25 24 23   7 6 5 4 3 2 1

British Library Cataloguing in Publication Data
A catalogue record for this book is available from the British Library.

ISBN 978-1-915046-76-5

Cover design by Angela Selfe
Art direction by Sarah Grace

Printed in the UK

Content

Introduction

Greetings

Thank you for opening this book. Hopefully you will stay with it to the last page.

Initial comments

Through the writing period we have been progressively aware that the subject is enormous. I write 'we' because as the author, I (Michael Wright) am indebted to others, on whose shoulders I stand, and feel I am often writing on their behalf. Who are we to try to encompass with our feeble words the biblical teachings concerning God the Holy Spirit? We are neither theologians nor well-known expositors of Scripture, but we feel an urge to share with others what we have learned, and in part experienced, of the blessed Paraclete.

You too probably long to know the Holy Spirit better; we pray that something in this book will spur you on in your pilgrimage. The Spirit himself will be your teacher, and it could well be that he will show you that, here and there, we have incorrectly, or inadequately, understood Scripture. Should this be the case, we suggest that you consult with others who evidently live in harmony with the Spirit and consistently manifest his fruit.

The gospel must be propagated; the world needs to hear that God is just, holy and love, that Jesus saves and that the Church must be prepared for Jesus' return: accomplishment will come about, but only 'by the Spirit'.

Potential readers

The primary aspiration of the trilogy is to encourage Christian readers to accord more time and effort into reading and searching the Scriptures, particularly in our case, with regard to the person and work of the Holy Spirit.

This concerns all generations, folk who are in the whole range of spiritual experience, development and growth, i.e. the newly born again, those who are keenly walking with and serving their Lord, those who are not so engaged, those who, for a variety of reasons, have many demands on their time and energy (including further education, apprenticeships, intensive professional commitments, family life, caring for elderly, disabled and suffering family members and others and so on), and also those who feel called to ministries which would benefit from full or part-time attendance at a Bible college.

We also have in mind local church leaders, who work full-time in their trade or profession, for whom we aspire to furnish useful material for ministry concerning God the Holy Spirit.

Teaching

The trilogy is centred on the theme of teaching, and since successful teaching involves much repetition, we ask our readers to tolerate the repetition they will find, including in the remaining books of the trilogy.

Bible versions

Except where otherwise indicated we have chosen to use and quote from the New International Version (NIV) of the Bible, 2011 UK version. Where other versions are used the following abbreviations indicate their identity:

- AV or KJV for the Authorized Version, or the King James Version.
- RV for the Revised Version, as used in quotes from The Century Bible commentary on the Gospel of John.
- NIV 1984 for older version of NIV.

References

The words to the hymns I referred to can be found at https://hymnary.org, unless an alternative source is specified in the text.

Acknowledgements

Firstly, I wish to mention the patience and support of my wife, Lucie. Other members of our family have helped, some from the start, others, particularly our daughter Danielle and her daughters Shirley and Clara, during the writing and editing of early drafts, along with typing. Our son Patrick has supported the enterprise throughout, particularly during the period of close collaboration with the publishers (final edit and publication). I am grateful for their support.

Michael Wright

1

Breath and Wind

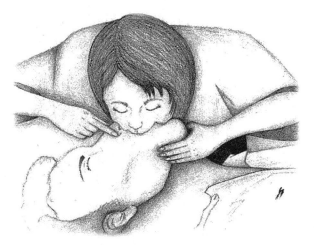

Breath

You have heard of it, maybe you have learned to practise it, you may have been witness to someone's life being saved by its use; we are thinking of mouth-to-mouth resuscitation. This is one of the most dramatic ways by which someone can sustain and save the life of another who has stopped breathing. Simply put, perhaps too simply, the practitioner inhales deeply, then exhales firmly by mouth into the opened mouth of the unconscious person, continuing in a regular rhythm until breathing returns. By this merciful act, one human's breath keeps another alive; without it, irreparable brain damage or death would ensue.

In all respects but one, the body of earth's first man was wonderfully complete. God had formed him from the inert dust of the ground. The bones, sinews and all the functional systems were present in Adam's body, but he was not alive. Genesis 2:7 tells us how God took his masterpiece the one indispensable step further; he 'breathed into his nostrils the breath [Hebrew *rûah*] of life, and the man became a living being'. So it was that the inanimate body of the first human being was quickened; the Creator's breath entered his lungs and all the vital systems became operational. What is more, it was by means of this sublime act that an intimate, sweet and unsullied relationship was established between the man and his Maker; profound mutual appreciation was the daily joy of God and man. The breath of God had established a oneness between the Living God and the living being. Cruden wrote about how Genesis 2:7 signifies the infusion by God of the soul into the body.[1] That man was immortal.

The Scriptures tell how this idyllic state changed dramatically. God's enemy engineered the temptation and fall of the 'living being', and the first man died spiritually; he was no longer in fellowship with his Maker; he was spiritually dead, due to his trespasses and sin, and this meant that he was alienated from God his Creator; Adam passed on this awful condition to all his descendants;

---

1. Alexander Cruden, *Cruden's Complete Concordance to the Old and New Testaments* (London: Morgan and Scott, undated); (Peabody, MA: Hendrickson, 1990; new edition), p. 48.

however, he was still alive physically, but mortal, and physical death was soon also to be his lot, and that of all his kind. The breath of God was no longer in man to the extent that it had been, but humans should be grateful to their Creator, for the residue of his breath that remains. Paul said as much to the Athenians: '[God] himself gives everyone life and breath and everything else' (Acts 17:25). Possession of this life-giving residue must be the basis of the universal human longing for God. This longing is often disguised in a multiplicity of ways, but is, nevertheless, everywhere present, often painfully so.

Humankind longs to be a 'living being' in the full sense that Adam was when he received the breath of God. The years during which we enjoy the presence of physical breath in our bodies should be regarded as years of hope and mercy; that which Job asserted so many millennia ago, mercifully remain true: 'In his [God's] hand is the life of every creature and the breath of all mankind' (Job 12:10). And while there's life, there's hope! Hope of experiencing the mercy of God, his pardon and the grace offered to us through his Son, Jesus Christ which, together with the action of the Spirit, combine to restore the divine breath in every part of our being, soul and spirit, as well as body.

We must pause now to note that Scripture associates the breath of God with the person and work of the Holy Spirit. To understand this, it seems preferable to begin our research in the New Testament where the Greek word *pneuma,* meaning breath, occurs very many times; in most cases it is translated 'spirit' or 'Spirit', the choice between the two possibilities being determined by the context; when translated 'Spirit' it is very often accompanied by the adjective 'Holy'. Here are just four examples: 'she was found to be pregnant through the Holy Spirit [breath]' (Matthew

1:18); 'baptising them in the name of the Father and of the Son and of the Holy Spirit [breath]' (Matthew 28:19); 'All of them were filled with the Holy Spirit [breath]' (Acts 2:4); 'hear what the Spirit [breath] says to the churches' (Revelation 2:7).

Pneuma figures frequently in everyday contemporary speech in many languages, i.e. in such words as pneumatic (air-filled) tyres, and pneumonia.

Another Greek word, *pnöe*, meaning blew, blows or wind, occurs only a few times in the New Testament, most notably, insofar as our present consideration is concerned, in John 3:8 where Jesus uses the word as a figure for the Spirit: 'The wind blows wherever it pleases . . . So it is with everyone born of the Spirit.'

Turning back to the Old Testament, with the benefit of the light of New Testament metaphorical usage of breath (*pneuma*) and wind (*pnöe*) for the Spirit, we can readily understand the Hebrew word *rûah*, also meaning breath, wind or spirit, as implying the Spirit of God or the Holy Spirit, when the context clearly indicates that it is the person of God that is meant. Let us revisit a handful of Old Testament scriptures which employ the breath metaphor for God the Holy Spirit:

- concerning creation: 'By the word of the LORD the heavens were made, their starry host by the breath of his mouth' (Psalm 33:6). The Word (suggesting the Son, cf. Hebrews 1:2), and the Spirit acted in unison, together with the Father, to bring all creation into being.

- giving life to the inanimate body of Adam; see earlier paragraphs for comment on Genesis 2:7.

- concerning all those who live on earth: 'God . . . who spreads out the earth . . . who gives breath to its people, and life to those who walk on it' (Isaiah 42:5). He who is breath gives physical breath to all humanity.

- a prayer for a return of old-time divine presence and blessing; 'Where is he who set his Holy Spirit (*rûah*) among them?' (Isaiah 63:11).

- in messianic prophecy: 'The Spirit [*rûah*] of the LORD will rest on him' (Isaiah 11:2), thus confirming that Jesus is the Christ, the Spirit-anointed One. The promised coming of the Spirit upon Jesus is presented both as a breathing and an anointing, two metaphors for the same empowering. Isaiah enunciates seven attributes of *rûah* that would be endowed on Messiah . . . abiding presence, 'wisdom', 'understanding', 'counsel', power, 'knowledge', 'fear of the LORD'.

From beginning to end, the Bible tells us of God's amazing plan of salvation and restoration for humanity; i.e. the restoration of all that was lost to Adam's fall, the consequences of which were subsequently made worse by his descendants wilful association with their first father's disobedience. The Scriptures provide many different images which explain God's plan and how he is bringing it to full accomplishment. Jesus Christ, in his entire person, and by his redemptive works, is at the heart of that plan. But Scripture also emphasises the importance of the person and actions of the Holy Spirit in restoring to persons and to peoples the breath of life, the *rûah*, the *pneuma*.

God's restoration intentions are stated or alluded to in numerous Old Testament passages. One of these is in Ezekiel 37:1-14. The prophet Ezekiel is in exile in Babylon with many of his Jewish compatriots. Jerusalem had been destroyed, her people deported. It was as if the nation of Israel had perished; they were like a scattering of dry and lifeless bones on the sun-baked floor of an arid valley. The nation no longer breathed; it was dead.

The hand of the LORD was on me, and he brought me out by the Spirit of the LORD and set me in the middle of a valley; it was full of bones. He led me to and fro among them, and I saw a great many bones on the floor of the valley, bones that were very dry. He asked me, 'Son of man, can these bones live?'

I said, 'Sovereign LORD, you alone know.'

Then he said to me, 'Prophesy to these bones and say to them, "Dry bones, hear the word of the LORD! This is what the Sovereign LORD says to these bones: I will make breath enter you, and you will come to life. I will attach tendons to you and make flesh come upon you and cover you with skin; I will put breath in you, and you will come to life. Then you will know that I am the LORD."'

So I prophesied as I was commanded. And as I was prophesying, there was a noise, a rattling sound, and the bones came together, bone to bone. I looked, and tendons and flesh appeared on them and skin covered them, but there was no breath in them.

Then he said to me, 'Prophesy to the breath; prophesy, son of man, and say to it, "This is what the Sovereign LORD says: come, breath, from the four winds and breathe into these slain, that they may live."' So I prophesied as he commanded me, and breath entered them; they came to life and stood up on their feet – a vast army.

Then he said to me: 'Son of man, these bones are the people of Israel. They say, "Our bones are dried up and our hope is gone; we are cut off." Therefore prophesy and say to them: "This is what the Sovereign LORD says: my people, I am going to open your graves and bring you up from them; I will bring you back to the land of Israel. Then you, my people, will know that I am the LORD, when I open your graves and bring you up from them. I will put my Spirit in you and you will live, and I will settle you in your own land. Then you will know that I the LORD have spoken, and I have done it, declares the LORD."'

The primary sense of this vividly descriptive prophetic text is that the exiles would return to Jerusalem, that the nation would be restored, and that this would come about through the Sovereign Lord breathing new life into Israel's then lifeless remains; lifeless, that is, at the time of the prophecy. Nevertheless, a much wider application of the principles enshrined in the prophecy is surely called for. Are there not today many valleys full of dry bones, in dire need of new life and restoration? What about present-day Israel, many present-day local churches, denominations, associations, countries and a multitude of individuals, including you and I, many of whom have known spiritual and moral health and fruitfulness in former times, but are today in poor health, dying or dead, and needing a prophet to say to them, 'Dry bones, hear the word of the LORD!'?

And that word will be a call to repentance which will be followed by an infusion of new breath, the Holy Spirit, the divine *pneuma,* bringing new life and restoration.

At the beginning of the twentieth century, the Church and chapel communities of the South Wales valleys were probably not spiritually dead or asleep, but they were dried up. Then God raised up a group of young people, with Evan Roberts as their leader, who ministered under an anointing of the Holy Spirit. They testified, Evan preached, the Spirit of God convicted many of sin and led them, young and old, into new life in Christ. God the Holy Spirit, the *pneuma,* breathed life into the newly converted, and renewed the older Christians who had become parched and dry. This was revival time in Wales and the Spirit outpouring, or in-breathing, flowed out into the remainder of the United Kingdom, Europe and more distant parts of the globe.

Through recent decades, many Catholic and Protestant communities have experienced a new in-breathing of spiritual life through what is commonly called the charismatic renewal. Some Christians are ill at ease with certain aspects of this movement, but most would acknowledge that its principle characteristics – renewed Christ-centredness in daily living, joy in service and worship, warmth in fellowship, zeal in witness and a lively appreciation of spiritual gifts and their use – have powerfully contributed to the quality and effectiveness of the communities directly concerned.

Many valleys full of dry bones remain. Is God asking us to reply to his question, 'Can these bones live'?

It is certainly important to recognise that the Holy Spirit, the breath of God, delights in restoring dynamic life in existing Christian communities and in establishing new ones; this is the story of the Acts of the Apostles. But the restoring and the establishing takes place on a personal level in each person within the communities. As God the Spirit breathed life into Adam's nostrils, so he breathes life into all whom he leads to an acceptance of Jesus as Saviour and Lord. Jesus described becoming a Christian as being born again (John 3:3); this essential first step into God's family is a new birth, and Jesus said that it is brought about by water (John 3:5), here representing the Word of God, and the Spirit, the *pneuma* or breath of God. This is the beginning, on an individual and personal level, of putting right and restoring all that had been lost due to the compounded sin of Adam and ourselves.

At the new birth, the Holy Spirit creates in the believer a new nature, Christ in us.

The work of restoration begins with a new birth and the placing of the newborn into their new family, the Church, the worldwide community of believers, the body of Christ. It is the Holy Spirit, the *pneuma*, who places, or baptises, the newborn into this blessed fellowship (1 Corinthians 12:13); here we have a delightful picture of the restorative work that the Holy Spirit effects; formerly lost, objects of wrath, excluded from the Eden of bliss, without hope, but now alive with Christ, breathing the breath of God, spiritually alive and incorporated into a community of love, grace and purpose, in which all 'were given the one Spirit to drink' (or breathe).

After the new birth, Jesus offers more of the Spirit's restorative power and grace to the newly born; as John the Baptist said, Jesus baptises with the Holy Spirit and with fire (Matthew 3:11). This he did for some 120 of his followers (disciples) on the Day of Pentecost, shortly after his ascension, when wind (breath) and fire were in evidence. This baptism, this in-breathing, wonderfully progressed the work of restoration in these men and women, taking them further on towards the spiritual maturity and adulthood that God must have intended for Adam and his kind. After the initial 120, multitudes of Christians, including those mentioned in the book of Acts, have been similarly baptised or breathed into, and these persons are conscious of the restorative work that the Spirit is taking forward in their lives and in their communities. They are also acutely aware of the reality that the Holy Spirit's work must always be regarded as ongoing. The restoration is not yet complete, for all Christians and all communities of Christians are still in the combat zone; on a personal level, the battle is still on between the two natures, old and new, which all believers possess – collectively too, between the 'children of light' (Ephesians 5:8) and the powers of darkness. The old nature with which we were born endeavours constantly to defile the new which we received with the new birth. Mercifully the Spirit is with us – indeed, in us – and he responds so faithfully to our call, breathing strength, renewal and restoration into our beings. His purpose is that we be 'living beings', in an even greater sense than Adam was.

Edwin Hatch[2] prayed in this way:

Breathe on me, Breath of God,
Fill me with life anew,
That I may love as Thou dost love,
And do what Thou wouldst do.

---

2. Edwin Hatch, 1835-39, 'Breathe on Me, Breath of God', https://library.timelesstruths. org/music/Breathe_on_Me_Breath_of_God/ (accessed 8.8.23).

Breathe on me, Breath of God,
Until my heart is pure,
Until with Thee I will one will,
To do and to endure.

Breathe on me, Breath of God,
Till I am wholly Thine,
Till all this earthly part of me
Glows with Thy fire divine.

Breathe on me Breath of God,
So, shall I never die,
But live with Thee the perfect life
Of Thine eternity.

Hugh Mitchell prayed rather differently, but with the same purpose and intensity:

Breath of Mount Calv'ry breathe upon me,
Refreshing wind of God's purity,
Sweep o'er my soul now setting me free,
Breath of Mount Calv'ry breathe upon me.[3]

John's account of Jesus appearing to his disciples during the evening of the day of his resurrection reads:

... when the disciples were together, with the doors locked for fear of the Jewish leaders, Jesus came and stood among them and said, 'Peace be with you!' After he said this, he showed them his hands and side. The disciples were overjoyed when they saw the Lord.

---

3.   Hugh Mitchell, 1914-2015 (Compiler), *Gospel Quintet Choruses, Book 1* (Gospel Quintet, 1942), song no 9.

Again Jesus said, 'Peace be with you! As the Father has sent me, I am sending you.' And with that he breathed on them and said, 'Receive the Holy Spirit. If you forgive anyone's sins, their sins are forgiven; if you do not forgive them, they are not forgiven.'

(John 20:19-23)

The full pouring out of the Spirit on the disciples had to be preceded by Jesus' ascension. Peter was inspired to explain this after the outpouring on the Day of Pentecost. How then was it possible for Jesus to do what he did fifty days before Pentecost? In what measure did Jesus transmit the Holy Spirit when he breathed on his disciples? These and other questions are easy to ask, but who can, who dare attempt an answer? For our part, we are content to note that when Jesus came to his friends, knowing them to be gripped by fear, he conveyed to them peace, showed them the marks of his wounds, gave them a very demanding commission ('I am sending you'), breathed on them the strengthening Spirit, and concluded by placing on them a very daunting responsibility (concerning the forgiveness of sins). Tenderly, thoughtfully, he breathed on them that they might receive the Holy Spirit, the Holy *Pneuma* or Breath. As it will be for the two witnesses, on some future day (see Revelation 11:1-12), so it was for the disciples who had been so devastated by the death of their Master, when he, newly risen from the dead, breathed on them new life and reassurance: 'the breath of life from God entered them, and they stood on their feet' (v. 11). Many believers today, behind closed doors, are receiving similar ministry from their risen Lord. The Holy Spirit is breathing on those who, perhaps for fear, or perhaps due to intense anticipation, have been holding their breath . . . the result being that they are breathing freely again.

A supremely important truth concerning the breath of God is outlined by the apostle Paul in his second letter to Timothy, his young friend and colleague:

All Scripture is God-breathed and is useful for teaching, rebuking, correcting and training in righteousness, so that the servant of God may be thoroughly equipped for every good work.'

(2 Timothy 3:16-17)

Wind

Cruden wrote:

The powerful operations and motions of God's Spirit, quickening or reviving the heart toward God, are compared to the blowing of the wind *(pnoë)*, John3.8. For as it is with the wind, man perceives it, by the effects of it, that there is such a thing, and that it does blow, yet his power cannot restrain it, neither can his reason enable him to know whence it rises, or from how far it comes, or how far it will reach; so is the spiritual change wrought in the soul; freely, where, in whom, when, and in what measure the Spirit pleases; and also powerfully, so as to make an evident sensible change, though the manner thereof be incomprehensible.[4]

None who are born again, of water and of the Spirit, fully understand either the word or the Spirit who have brought

---

4. Cruden, *Cruden's Complete Concordance to the Old and New Testaments*, p. 685.

about this wonder, but they are deeply aware of the effects, just as they are of the wind that blows their way, while only feebly understanding its origin, destination and mechanics. Believers feel the impact of the Spirit: 'The Spirit himself testifies with our spirit that we are God's children' (Romans 8:16).

Wind and fire are both used in Scripture as metaphors of God's actions, including the works of God the Holy Spirit. In his second letter to Timothy, Paul uses both metaphors to encourage his younger co-worker: 'I remind you to fan into flame the gift of God, which is in you through the laying on of my hands' (2 Timothy 1:6). Fanning is obviously a person-generated movement of air, but here it can certainly be understood to be the harnessing by Timothy of the *pnoë* of the Spirit. What a pleasure it is to see flames jumping joyfully upward from the dying embers we have energetically fanned! Paul's practical counsel is appropriate for all his readers.

A stimulating and useful exercise we can undertake is to give everyday sayings concerning wind a Christian connotation and to apply the result to a current circumstance:

- As disciples we are long-distance runners, determined to stay the course, but plagued, from time to time, by weariness, bad weather or 'stitch' . . . oh, for a second breath, we sigh; it comes; we feel the renewed energy, and press on for the finishing line. 'Be filled with the Spirit', Paul would say to us, a second, a third time, every day, today!

- It could be that in accordance with a conviction that God has given to us as a local church we have embarked, as if on a voyage of discovery, on the evangelism of a district, or some other form of ministry; we had made good progress, but now progress is slow, seemingly non-existent; we are in a doldrum . . . oh, for wind in our sails! In ourselves, or our group, or our local church, we haven't enough breath to move our gospel boat 1m forward, but the wind of the Spirit, who has propelled the vessel over seas and oceans, through centuries past, has lost none of his energy (*dynamis*, Acts 1:8); our role is to hoist the sails (this may include looking again at our motives, and repentance may well be necessary), and then ask the Spirit to fill them.

- Brother Lawrence (circa 1611-91), the French Carmelite lay brother and mystic, left us this thought: 'Those who have the gale of the Spirit go forward even in sleep.'[5] This is my prayer: 'Lord, teach us to hoist our sails, and to experience the propulsion of a following wind (of the Spirit), and when the winds are contrary, to tack into them.'

---

5. Brother Lawrence, *The Practice of the Presence of God* (London: Hodder & Stoughton, 1981).

- Some people like them, others don't, but their numbers are growing, and will continue to do so. Wind farms are onshore and offshore, and their turbines are producing more and more electricity, green energy at that. Is it too much to suggest that God has equipped his Church with 'blades' which, by rotation, are able to harness the energy of the Spirit, which is then distributed both within and without the community of believers, in order to empower, convince, convict, heal and progress the kingdom?

- Andrew Reed prayed to God the Holy Spirit:

  Come as the wind, with rushing sound
  and Pentecostal grace,
  that all of woman born may see
  the glory of your face.[6]

---

6. Andrew Reed, 1787-1862, 'Spirit Divine, Attend Our Prayers', https://hymnary.org/hymn/HGSP2008/583 (accessed 8.8.23).

The adjective *pneumatikos,* meaning spiritual, is an important derivative of *pneuma* and occurs in a number of New Testament passages, all in the letters, where it conveys the notion of Spirit-breathed life and grace present in, for example, the gifts spoken of in 1 Corinthians 12, and the songs in Ephesians 5:19.

1 Corinthians 12:1: 'Now about the gifts of the Spirit [or 'the spirituals', the *pneumatikos*], brothers and sisters, I do not want you to be uninformed.'

Ephesians 5:19: 'Speaking to one another with psalms, hymns, and songs from the Spirit [the *pneumatikos*].'

2

Fire

Statements in Scripture which tell us that God is a fire are few, but clearly they are very important; one feels that they are to be understood as being figurative, in meaning and purpose; I am aware of just two, Deuteronomy 4:24, where Moses declares 'the LORD your God is a consuming fire, a jealous God' and Hebrews 12:29, 'worship God acceptably with reverence and awe, for our God is a consuming fire'. This, one feels, sets an awesome tone to our meditation on fire as a metaphor for the Holy Spirit.

Both Matthew (3:11) and Luke (3:16) relate John Baptist's prophecy concerning the soon to begin ministry of Jesus with these words 'He will baptise you with the Holy Spirit *and fire*' (my emphasis). Many Bible scholars consider that the *fire* aspect of this prophecy concerns the judgement that all Christians will experience after Christ's return. Several passages inform us of this coming burning which will consume the inadequate, unChristlike, 'wood, hay or straw' (1 Corinthians 3:12) – as works we have practised during our lifetime; see 1 Corinthians 3:10-15,

2 Corinthians 5:10 and Romans 14:10; the latter passage says that 'we will all stand before God's judgment seat'. At that time all the residual impurities will be burnt up. We cannot imagine that this will be an enjoyable experience, but our loving Father will carry us through, and he gives us the courage in the here and now to acknowledge that he is so wonderfully kind and good to have planned such a necessary fire. So, it will be that each believer's works will be put to the test by God's fire, 'so that each of us may receive what is due to us for the things done while in the body, whether good or bad' (2 Corinthians 5:10). The question we must ask is this: is it to this judgement fire that John's prophecy refers?

Surely there is another way to understand what this prophetic word is telling us about the Holy Spirit and fire. John's task was to prepare the way for Jesus to begin and then to carry out his three years or so of ministry, which would involve presenting and revealing his person to his contemporaries, particularly his disciples, teaching, healing, delivering and unveiling to open hearts the person and nature of his Father. Throughout this period, Jesus would be on the road that would lead to his great redemptive work at Calvary, followed by his all-victorious resurrection and his sublime ascension, shortly after which he would accomplish a great act of grace by pouring out the promised Holy Spirit on the waiting believers. John's prophetic ministry foresaw all that happened up to and including the Day of Pentecost, and indeed from that Day on through to the end of the period foreseen by God for the proclamation of the gospel. The principal truths that John proclaimed about Jesus are in Scripture in order to enlighten people throughout the period which will conclude with Christ's return, the two leading truths being, firstly, that Jesus is 'the Lamb of God, who takes away the sin of the world' (John 1:29) and, secondly, that he it is who 'will baptise you with the Holy Spirit and fire' (Matthew 3:11). All that is taught in these declarations, and the blessings promised, are for people during the here and now of their time on earth.

It follows that a baptism of fire is God's plan for believers during their lifetime on earth. Furthermore, it seems to be wrong to separate baptism with the Holy Spirit from baptism with fire. Surely the unfolding story through the book of Acts shows, in more ways than one, that the two are one and the same, the fire aspect placing an emphasis on a very important element of the Spirit's work in believers, and in the entire body of Christ.

Here are a few citations from commentaries (on Matthew 3:11 in the AV):

Alexander Cruden

God hath often appeared in fire and encompassed with fire; as when he showed himself in the burning bush, and descended on Mount Sinai in the midst of flames, thundering, and lighting, Exod.3.2.[7]

The angel of the Lord appeared to Moses in the burning bush and the mountain was covered in smoke (Exodus 19:18). He would also show himself to his prophets Isaiah, Ezekiel and John either in the midst of fire (Isaiah 6:4; Ezekiel 1:4) or incorporating fire in himself (Revelation 1:14).

It is the work of the Holy Spirit to enlighten, purify and sanctify the soul, and to enflame it with love for God and

---

7. Cruden, *Cruden's Complete Concordance to the Old and New Testaments*, p 203.

zeal for his glory.

Is it not true to assert that the fire appearances of God described in the Old Testament should be understood as being manifestations of deity in his three indivisible persons, Father, Son and Holy Spirit? It follows that we should have no difficulty in associating Spirit baptism with fire baptism.

Matthew Henry

It is Christ's prerogative to baptise with the Holy Ghost. This he did in the extraordinary gifts of the Spirit conferred upon the apostles. This he does in the graces and comforts of the Spirit given to them that ask him. They who are baptised with the Holy Ghost are baptized as with fire. Is fire enlightening? So the Spirit is a Spirit of illumination. Is it warming? And do not their hearts burn within them? Is it consuming? And does not the Spirit of judgement, as a Spirit of burning, consume the dross of their corruptions? Does fire make all it seizes like itself? And does it move upwards? So, does the Spirit make the soul holy like itself, and its tendency is heaven-ward.[8]

Jamieson, Fausset and Brown

... and with fire. To take this as a distinct baptism from that of the Spirit – a baptism of the impenitent in hell-fire – is exceedingly unnatural. Yet this was the view

---

8. Matthew Henry's Commentary on the Whole Bible, Complete and Unabridged in One Volume (Peabody MA: Hendrickson Publishers, 1991), p. 1619.

of Origen among the Fathers; and among moderns, of Neander, Meyer, De Wette and Lange. Nor was it much better to refer it to the fire of the great day, by which the earth and the works that are therein shall be burned up. Clearly, as we think, it is but the fiery character of the Spirit's operations upon the soul – searching, consuming, refining, sublimating – as nearly all good interpreters understand the words.[9]

Adam Clarke

That the influences of the Spirit of God are here designed needs but little proof. Christ's religion was to be a spiritual religion, and was to have its seat in the heart. Outward precepts, however well they might describe, could not produce inward spirituality. This was the province of the Spirit of God, and of him alone; therefore, he is represented here under the similitude of fire, because he was to illuminate and invigorate the soul, penetrate every part, and assimilate the whole to the image of the God of glory.[10]

G. Campbell Morgan

Campbell Morgan's commentary embraces verses 10-12 of Matthew chapter 3:

Listen to what John says about [Jesus'] methods. This is to be a strange and wonderful King who is

9.   Jamieson, Fausset & Brown, *Commentary Practical and Explanatory on the Whole Bible* (London: Oliphants Ltd, 1961), p. 888.
10. Adam Clarke, *Commentary on Matthew* (Pokeno, NZ: Titus Books, 2013), Kindle Edition, location 814.

coming. He is to be destructive and constructive in His method; and His victories are to be destructive and constructive.

His methods of destruction are, 'the axe,' 'the fan,' and 'the fire.' 'The axe is laid unto the root of the trees,' said John. It is ready. He is coming, and His 'fan is in His hand,' the fan that winnows. And the fire will burn.

But His methods are constructive. He shall baptize you with fire; He shall cleanse the threshing floor, not destroy it, and He will 'gather His wheat into the garner.' Mark the contrast. The axe at the root of the trees for destruction for the cutting off of the fruitless; the fan for scattering the chaff; the fire for immediately devouring the chaff. But mark the constructive work. The fire is for cleansing and energy; the cleansing of the threshing-floor, that perfect work may go forward, and the garnering and the gathering in of the wheat. It is the same thing, and the same instrument that does two opposite things. The fan drives away the chaff, leaving the wheat. The fire burns up the thing that cannot stand its fierce flame; and perfects that which can bear the flame. And so the King Who comes is to be destructive and constructive – destructive, for the fruitless tree is to be hewn down; the chaff is to be driven away and burnt, constructive, for the threshing-floor is to be cleansed; the wheat is to be gathered and garnered, and men are to be fire-baptized.[11]

---

11.   George Campbell Morgan, *The Gospel According to Matthew* (Eugene, OR: Wipf & Stock Publishers, 2017), p. 24.

The fan here is a fork-like tool used to separate harvested grain from its chaff.

Each of the several biblical metaphors for the Holy Spirit is stimulating, readily touching our minds and our hearts, and that of 'fire' is particularly invigorating for it easily presents us with a number of the operations which the Spirit habitually carries out, some being destructive, others transforming and empowering. Some of these are highlighted by the commentators quoted above.

I well remember my first science lesson at secondary school; our teacher said, 'Man can neither create (from nothing), nor destroy (to leave nothing); he can only transform.' No mention was made as to whether a particular transformation could be good or bad; clearly both are possible, and humanity's responsibility is clearly engaged. Being God, the Holy Spirit participated in the creation work; being God, he is also able to destroy, as G. Campbell Morgan points out in his comments on Matthew 3:10-12. But the burning work in the lives of Christians during the present dispensation has mostly to do with transforming and enabling, and it is always good. To do these things must be a great delight to the Spirit, the Father and the Son.

That fire transforms is common knowledge. It is combustion or burning, in which substances combine with oxygen from the air and typically give out bright light, heat and smoke i.e. combine with oxygen to become something different, that is transformed. So, the fire of the Spirit operates to transform a sinner into a saint, a coward – such as Peter was – into a courageous, unwavering witness, and an uncertain and apprehensive group of believers into an assured and purposeful band of 'all for Jesus' mission-minded disciples.

The fire in a steam locomotive burns fuel, transforming it chemically and so liberating heat, which in turn changes the water in the system into steam, which moves the engine's driving mechanisms, and then, with a toot and a whistle, the train is on its way! Success is due, initially, to the expertise of the locomotive's designers, then to the diligence of the manufacturers, and finally to the skill of the driver and his mate. At every stage a controlled and harnessed fire is envisaged, and oh, what pleasure success brings to all concerned; witness the continued use of these engineering masterpieces for recreational purposes and, in some parts of the world, as public railway workhorses. Maybe I am being over nostalgic, but this is worthwhile if it stimulates desire to experience within the Church the mighty, controlled power of the fire of the Spirit.

No doubt there have been many instances when the Spirit has intervened to completely burn up an offering, a project, an object. Immediately we think of that which God did one day on Mount Carmel (1 Kings 18). Elijah puts an amazing challenge to Baal's prophets: 'The god who answers by fire – he is God' (v. 24). Baal does not answer his prophets' agonising pleas. No reply, no fire. Elijah steps forward and calls out:

LORD, the God of Abraham, Isaac and Israel, let it be known today that you are God in Israel and that I am your servant and have done all these things at your command. Answer me, LORD, answer me, so these people will know that you, LORD, are God, and that you are turning their hearts back again.

(vv. 36-37)

God responds – 'the fire of the LORD fell and burned up the sacrifice, the wood, the stones and the soil, and also licked up the water in the trench' (v. 38).

On multiple occasions the Spirit of God has fallen like fire on the offering, the difficulty, the apparent need, that his people have presented to him, burning up, consuming completely whatever it was, in order to bring about a new and entirely different situation. In this light we can perhaps understand what happened in England during the period immediately after the martyrdom of Bible translator William Tyndale in 1536 at Vilvoorde in Flanders. Anti-Christian fire consumed Tyndale's body, but the fire of the Spirit used this apparent tragedy to accelerate the momentum that led shortly to the coming into being of the Authorised Version of the Bible, substantially based on Tyndale's work, and also the placing of a copy of the Bible, in English, in every parish church in the land. The energy that the Spirit of fire generates continues, to this day, to take forward the work of translating the Scriptures into the languages in which the Bible is, as yet, not available.

We also remember with gratitude bishops Hugh Latimer and Nicholas Ridley who died together at the stake in 1555 at Oxford. Latimer's amazingly prophetic encouragement for his friend was 'Be of good cheer, Master Ridley, and play the man. We shall this day light such a candle, by God's grace, in England, as I trust shall never be put out.'[12] Surely God was with his servants in that terrible fire, and the Spirit of fire saw to it that in the coming years, and centuries, a wonderfully creative, transforming work of grace would spread through England, the British Isles and also to distant

12. www.bartleby.com/lit-hub/samuel-arthur-bent/hugh-latimer-2/ (accessed 8.8.23).

parts of the globe. The bodies of many of God's servants, women and men, have been reduced to ashes, but the constructive fire of the Spirit has transformed the cinders into church building blocks and into many, many candles which have, and still are, spreading gospel light into dark places. Maybe some of our plans and ambitions should go through the fire too.

In the 1950s, a Bible institute in Burgess Hill in the south of England was deeply in debt; students and staff prayed earnestly, seeking the face of God. The Holy Spirit came down upon them, and a spiritual awakening was experienced. On a visit, I noted a small commemorative plaque, placed in the prayer room, states 'The fire of the Lord fell and burned up the debt'.

Harry Tee penned this hymn which we can make our prayer:

They were gathered in an upper chamber,
as commanded by the risen Lord,
and the promise of the Father
there they sought with one accord,
when the Holy Ghost from heaven descended
like a rushing wind and tongues of fire:
so dear Lord, we seek Thy blessing,
come with glory now our hearts inspire.

Let the fire fall, let the fire fall,
let the fire from heaven fall;
we are waiting and expecting,
now in faith, dear Lord, we call;
let the fire fall, let the fire fall,
on Thy promise we depend;

from the glory of Thy presence
let the Pentecostal fire descend.[13]

The second verse of the hymn takes the reader to Mount Carmel, and Elijah's call for divine intervention, the third tells of the covenant spelt out in Acts 2:39, and the fourth invites believers to ask of God: 'With a living coal from off Thy altar touch our lips to swell Thy wondrous praise' (see Isaiah 6:4-9).

We have already noted that Holy Spirit fire does not always consume or burn up. We recall the amazing sight that Moses, the shepherd, was privileged to witness while he was working not far from Mount Horeb. He saw a bush engulfed in flames; not unusual in a hot, parched terrain, but here the great difference was this: 'it did not burn up' (Exodus 3:2)! Moses came closer to the flames, but he was not scorched; then God called to him by name from within the bush, telling him not to 'come any closer', and continuing with these majestic words of divine authority and commission:

Take off your sandals, for the place where you are standing is holy ground . . . I am the God of your father, the God of Abraham, the God of Isaac and the God of Jacob . . . I have indeed seen the misery of my people in Egypt. I have heard them crying out because of their slave drivers, and I am concerned about their suffering . . . So now, go. I am sending you to Pharaoh to bring my people the Israelites out of Egypt.

(Exodus 3:5-10)

---

13. Harry Tee, ?-1959, 'Let the Fire Fall', www.godsongs.net/2021/05/let-the-fire-fall-they-were-gathered-in-an-upper-chamber.html (accessed 8.8.23).

The rest of this extraordinary dialogue can be read in Exodus 3, including the beautiful revelation, by God, of his name. God said to Moses, 'I AM WHO I AM. This is what you are to say to the Israelites: I AM has sent me to you' (v. 14).

Every generation of Christians is commissioned to proclaim, in Jesus' name, liberty for those in slavery to God's enemy, and furthermore to exercise ministries of deliverance, also in Christ's name. It is the Holy Spirit, the Spirit of fire, who equips for such endeavours. Maybe for the remainder of his days Moses felt like that bush, vulnerable and powerless, yet graciously enveloped by the non-consuming but enabling fire of God. Weak and fragile as we are, as the body of Christ is, the loving, non-consuming strength of the Holy Spirit, the Spirit of fire, is longing to enflame us, in order that we might be used to bring liberation and deliverance in a very needy world.

On the Day of Pentecost, the waiting believers began to hear and feel the tangible presence of the Holy Spirit, that the ascended Son of God had received from the Father and was pouring out on them. 'They saw what seemed to be tongues of fire that separated and came to rest on each of them' (Acts 2:3). It is usually assumed that it was on their heads that the tongues of fire reposed. The recipients did not suffer burns, but we can assume that their minds were enlightened, and that their hearts were more than warmed. The energy and empowering of the Spirit were suddenly becoming an amazing reality in their personal and collective experience. The remainder of the book of Acts explains the consequences.

In their first letter to the Thessalonian Christians the apostolic trio, Paul, Silas and Timothy, wrote: 'Do not quench the Spirit. Do not treat prophecies with contempt'

(1 Thessalonians 5:19-20). Here we learn that it is possible for Christians to extinguish the fire kindled by the Spirit. Our common experiences tell us that fire can be put out in several ways, for example by spreading the dying embers rather than feeding them, by using water, dampeners, chemical powders or some other means of starving the fire of oxygen. Each of us can readily spiritualise all of this. Suffice it to acknowledge that all believers should avoid putting out the Spirit's fire in their own lives, the lives of others and their local church. On the contrary, we can contribute to the maintenance of the Spirit's fire by walking in close company with Jesus, thereby feeding fuel and oxygen to the fire. Furthermore, instead of being contemptuous of prophetic ministry, whether it be proclamation or prediction, Christians can please the Spirit by welcoming the prophetic word and acting upon it. In the light of the first chapter of the first letter to the Thessalonians, where the writers paint a glowing picture of the young church and its effective outreach, it is surprising that the trio were inspired to exhort the community to not extinguish the fire of the Spirit. Evidently they needed, and we too need, to avoid complacency and all the influences within our fellowships and without, and in our natures, that seek to want a more comfortable life than that of being a burning bush.

Fire often has a cleansing, purifying effect. Even a forest fire, destructive as it usually is, can have a medium and long-term beneficial effect, due to the elimination of dead wood, the reinvigoration of the soil and the opportunity given for new, healthy growth to come through. The refiner's fire separates the useful, in some cases precious, metal from the ore and the dross; through the millennia of effort and discovery, using fire, humanity has learned to acquire and appreciate iron, copper, tin, silver, gold and all the rest.

Cleansing, sanctifying and making whole by the fire of the Spirit are realities which have been longed for, and experienced, by God-fearing people before and after the Day of Pentecost. In order to obtain pure metals, very high temperatures are necessary; the process is not easy; it is not comfortable. It is said that purity is achieved when the surface of the molten silver or gold reflects to the refiner a clear image of his face.

Malachi prophesied:

> But who can endure the day of his coming? Who can stand when he appears? For he will be like a refiner's fire or a launderer's soap. He will sit as a refiner and purifier of silver; he will purify the Levites and refine them like gold and silver. Then the LORD will have men who will bring offerings in righteousness, and the offerings of Judah and Jerusalem will be acceptable to the LORD, as in days gone by, as in former years.
>
> *(Malachi 3:2-4)*

Malachi tells us that this will happen when the 'messenger of the covenant ... will come' (Malachi 3:1), that is, when the Messiah comes. And come he has! As he promised he has given his people the Holy Spirit, and an important aspect of Spirit baptism is the fire that refines. A consequence of the New Testament teaching of the priesthood of all believers (1 Peter 2:9) is that the fulfilment of Malachi's prophecy during the Church period means that it is God's will that the Holy Spirit be invited by every child of God, i.e. every 'priest', to affect his fiery, refining, transforming work in their lives, and in their local churches.

The day had been full, tiring and satisfying; night was falling; a slight chill was setting in, and word went around to be off to the nearby wood in search of tinder for the fire. Soon the lads returned with arms full of suitable tinder, and not long after they were in a rough circle around a cheerfully crackling campfire; the dancing, jumping, ever-changing flames were soon having a hypnotic effect on each and all; none wanted to resist gazing at the blazing pile of joy, while at the same time drinking hot chocolate, munching currant buns, telling yarns and singing, raucously, but not tunefully, well-worn, but greatly enjoyed songs. Such noble thoughts as the character and lifelong friendship building value to what they were experiencing entered few, perhaps none, of their minds, but the warmth and exuberance generated by that fire was having a long-term, durable and beneficial effect.

The Holy Spirit is he who warms, comforts and constantly renews the joy and contentment of Christians and their communities. Christians are accustomed to gazing upon Jesus, and are thereby wonderfully blessed. Why not gaze on the Spirit too? For he, with the Son, is the fire around whom we are gathered; oh, how comforting, relaxing and uniting it is to gaze into the fire of God. One thing is certain – if we look expectantly to the Spirit, we shall rapidly find that our gaze is diverted to the Father's beloved Son. We will remember that Jesus said, 'He will not speak on his own . . . He will glorify me because it is from me that he will receive what he will make known to you' (John 16:13-14).

Romans 14:17 says 'the kingdom of God is not a matter of eating and drinking, but of righteousness, peace and joy in the Holy Spirit'.

The Holy Spirit is the Christian's comforter, he who brings warmth and assurance; Jesus said, in John 14:16-17: 'And I will pray the Father, and he shall give you another Comforter, that he may abide with you for ever; Even the Spirit of truth' (KJV).

Inspired by this promise, Harriet Auber gave us these beautiful words to sing:

Our blest Redeemer, ere He breathed
His tender last farewell,
A Guide, a Comforter, bequeathed
With us to dwell.[14]

Thinking along a rather different track, the story comes to memory of a congregation of early Methodists who were assembled for worship on what was probably a chilly day. They were gathered around a fire but, more importantly, they had another fire in their hearts. So, they sang, and did so while dancing around the fire. Their worship song was, as I recollect it:

The Lamb, the Lamb, the bleeding Lamb,
I love the sound of Jesu's name,
It gets my spirit all in a flame,
Glory to the bleeding Lamb![15]

When, in a particular way, the Spirit of fire reveals to believers the person and work of Christ, it is not surprising that their spirits become enflamed.

---

14. Harriet Auber, 1773-1862, 'Our Blest Redeemer', https://hymnary.org/text/our_blest_redeemer_ere_he_breathed (accessed 8.8.23).
15. Hodgson Casson (1788-1851), 'The Bleeding Lamb', https://hymnary.org/text/my_savior_suffered_on_the_tree (accessed 8.8.23).

Ephesians 5:18-19 says, 'be filled with the Spirit, speaking to one another with psalms, hymns, and songs from the Spirit. Sing and make music from your heart to the Lord'. The word 'heart' is in the singular, from which we might understand that the heart of the community is meant; in the unity of the Spirit, they were to sing as with one heart.

The Wesley brothers placed strong emphasis on the person and work of the Holy Spirit. This magnificent hymn, written by Charles, does not mention the Spirit, but the whole tenor of the brothers' ministries encourages us to understand that the fire of which Charles writes comes jointly from the Christ and the Comforter:

O thou who camest from above,
the pure celestial fire to impart,
kindle a flame of sacred love
on the mean altar of my heart!

There let it for thy glory burn
with inextinguishable blaze,
and trembling to its source return return
in humble prayer and fervent praise.

Jesus, confirm my heart's desire
to work, and speak, and think for thee;
still let me guard the holy fire,
and still stir up thy gift in me.

Ready for all thy perfect will,
my acts of faith and love repeat,
till death thy endless mercies seal,
and make the sacrifice complete.[16]

---

16. Charles Wesley, 1707-88, 'Thou Who Camest from Above', https://hymnary.org/text/o_thou_who_camest_from_above (accessed 8.8.23).

God the Holy Spirit confirms to the believer's heart and mind Jesus' work of grace, and his call, that is the believer's place in the New Covenant that God established between himself and the redeemed, on the basis of the atonement achieved by Jesus' sacrificial death. Genesis 15 beautifully relates that part of God's covenant with Abram, which concerned the promise of extensive territory. Abram had prepared an offering of animals and birds; the animals he cut in half and, with the whole birds, he set out the entire offering in two rows, and fell into a deep sleep! Then, 'When the sun had set and darkness had fallen, a smoking brazier with a blazing torch appeared and passed between the pieces' (v. 17). What a delightful introduction for Abram to the promises that God was about to make to him and his descendants. Is this not a figure of Jesus' sacrificial offering of himself, and of the offering of praise and worship by the disciples gathered on the Day of Pentecost, to which the response from on high was the sending down of the Spirit of fire . . . 'tongues of fire that separated and came to rest on each of them' (Acts 2:3), thus confirming the New Covenant, particularly the territorial/all nations aspects? Peter was inspired to declare 'the promise [of forgiveness for the repentant followed by the gift of the Holy Spirit] is for you and your children and for all who are far off—for all whom the Lord our God will call' (v. 39).

Surely the sight of the blazing torch stayed with Abram for the rest of his days. The fire of the Spirit abides in and upon the body of Christ.

Having briefly commented on several of the fire-related aspects of the Holy Spirit's works, we should return to the foundational truth stated in Hebrews 12:29: 'our "God is a consuming fire".' This statement clearly implies that God in his three persons, Father, Son and Holy Spirit, is a consuming fire; the writer exhorts us to bear this very much in mind when we worship.

3

Dove

From time to time, during my childhood and teenage years, I accompanied my mother who regularly attended the services of the local Methodist church. The congregational singing was inspiring, and that of the choir left me with rich and abiding memories. I particularly remember these words sung by choir and soloist to a hauntingly beautiful melody:

Oh, for the wings, for the wings of a dove,
Far away, far away, would I rove! . . .

In the wilderness build me a nest,
and remain there forever at rest[17]

This is a metrical version of Psalm 55:6-8, which is generally understood to have been written by Israel's king David when he was in danger to those who were conspiring

---

17. Felix Mendelssohn, 1809-47, 'O For the Wings of a Dove', www.jiosaavn.com/lyrics/ mendelssohn%3A-o-for-the-wings-of-a-dove-lyrics/RB8hRllzQgE (accessed 8.8.23).

against him. In this light the imagery is easily understood; however, for me the picture is perplexing. Is not the dove a very sociable bird, almost always to be seen in a flock, finding security and acceptance among fellow creatures? How come, then, this longing to get away from kindred company, to be alone in a desert, of all places? What an unnatural demeanour for dove and king to be forced to adopt. The non-acceptance, and total absence of security they felt, must have been overwhelming. Most of us, for a host of different reasons, have at some time expressed our feelings in a similar manner to David. Have we thought of doing so by associating our aspirations with the dove-like Spirit?

David's heart-breaking exclamation speaks to us of how his 'Greater Son', Jesus, he who among men was as meek as a dove, must have felt when the conspirator's net was tightening around him; the temptation was there to escape, to get away from it all, but the temptation was resisted, and he stayed among his enemies in order to bear the full fury of their hatred.

Taking a different line of approach, Scripture makes it clear to us that the dove-like Holy Spirit, he who delights in fostering concord, fellowship and the 'flock' ideal among believers, he who strives to open hard hearts to the love and grace of God will, if grieved, take to the wing . . . he returns, of course, when the grief is confessed and pardon is requested.

The picture in Psalm 55 stands as a warning to persons, communities and denominations that the Spirit of God, while being all-powerful, is very sensitive. He will flee if grieved. This was David's cry: 'Oh, that I had the wings of a dove! I would fly away and be at rest. I would flee far away and stay in the desert; I would hurry to my place of shelter, far from the tempest and storm' (vv. 6-8).

Whether or not we have difficulty with the dove imagery expressed by David, we probably have no problems at all with the dove metaphor when applied elsewhere in Scripture to the person of the Holy Spirit. Perhaps 'metaphor' is not the right word, for each of the Gospel writers state that at Jesus' baptism the Holy Spirit manifested himself in the form of a dove. Matthew wrote:

As soon as Jesus was baptised, he went up out of the water. At that moment heaven was opened, and he saw the Spirit of God descending like a dove and alighting on him. And a voice from heaven said, 'This is my Son, whom I love; with him I am well pleased.'
(Matthew 3:16-17)

And John's account reads: 'Then John [the Baptist] gave this testimony: "I saw the Spirit come down from heaven as a dove and remain on him"' (John 1:32). It seems to be certain that the dove seen by Jesus and John was a real physical bird, not an image or a vision. Jesus, of course, understood perfectly the implications of the manifestation, and John's grasp of its sense must have been very complete too, for, in addition to the divine revelation he no doubt received, the ambient culture of his day attributed to the dove similar qualities and attributes as those recognised more or less universally today. Then as now the dove was regarded as embodying meekness, purity, simplicity, guilelessness and harmlessness. Here are a few extracts from commentaries:

The Century Bible commentary on John 1:32 (RV) reads:

The fitness of the symbol arose from the fact that the dove was accounted sacred in the East as the emblem of brooding, fostering love (cf. Gen. viii. 9-11, where it appears as a messenger of peace), and was therefore an appropriate sign of the full and unreserved communication of divine grace bestowed upon Jesus at his baptism, and which he was to impart to others, baptising with the Holy Ghost.[18]

Matthew Henry on the account in Matthew's Gospel (Matthew 3:16, KJV):

If there must be a bodily shape (Lu. 3:22), it must not be that of a man. None therefore was more fit than the shape of one of the fowls of heaven (heaven being now opened), and of all fowls none was so significant as the shape of a dove. (1) The Spirit of Christ is a dove-like spirit. . . . The Spirit descended, not in the shape of an eagle, which is, though a royal bird, yet a bird of prey, but in the shape of a dove, compared to whom no creature is more harmless and inoffensive. Such must Christians be, harmless as doves. The dove mourns much (Isa. 38:14). Christ often wept; and penitent souls are compared to doves of the valleys. (2) The dove was the only fowl that was offered in sacrifice (Lev. 1:14), and Christ offered himself without spot to God. (3) The tidings of the decrease of Noah's flood were brought by a dove, with an olive-leaf in her mouth: fitly therefore are the glad tidings of peace with God brought by the Spirit as a dove. That God was in Christ reconciling the world to himself, is a joyful message, which comes to us upon the wing, the wings of a dove.[19]

---

18. *The Century Bible, St John* (J.A. McClymont, ed.; Edinburgh: T.C. & E.C. Jack, 1910), p. 126.
19. Matthew Henry, p. 1621.

Jamieson, Fausset and Brown, also on Matthew 3:16 (KJV):

'But why in this form? The scripture use of this emblem will be our best guide here. 'My dove, my undefiled one,' says the Song of Solomon (6:9). This is chaste purity. Again, 'Be harmless as doves,' says Christ himself (Matt. 10:16); this is the same thing, in the form of inoffensiveness towards men. 'A conscience void of offence toward God and toward men' (Acts 24:16) expresses both. Further, when we read in the Song (2:14), 'O my dove, that art in the *clefts* of the rocks, in the *secret places* of the stairs . . . , let me see thy countenance, let me hear thy voice; for sweet is thy voice, and thy countenance is comely' – it is shrinking modesty, meekness, gentleness, that is thus charmingly depicted. In a word – not to allude to the historical emblem of the dove that flew back to the ark, bearing in its mouth the olive leaf of peace (Gen. 8:11) – when we read (Ps. 68:13) 'Ye shall be as the wings of a dove covered with silver, and her feathers with yellow gold,' it is beauteousness that is thus held forth. And was not such that 'holy, harmless, undefiled one,' the 'separate from sinners'? 'Thou art fairer than the children of men: grace is poured into thy lips; therefore, God hath blessed thee for ever!' But the fourth gospel gives us one more piece of information here, on the authority of one who saw and testified of it: 'John bare record, saying I saw the Spirit descending from heaven like a dove, and IT ABODE UPON HIM.'.[20]

Following these citations from the works of our learned brethren, here are a few personal thoughts on Matthew

---

20. Jamieson, Fausset & Brown, p. 889.

3:16 which reads: 'As soon as Jesus was baptised, he went up out of the water. At that moment heaven was opened, and he [Jesus or John] saw the Spirit of God descending like a dove and alighting on him.'

'Heaven was opened'

Mark wrote 'torn open' (Mark 1:10); the occasion was momentous, for it is not every day that heaven opens in this dramatic way. The Bible tells of several moments when heaven opened to humans in a visible manner.

One day Ezekiel was among his fellow exiles by the Kebar river, south of Babylon, when 'the heavens were opened' and, as he afterwards wrote, 'I saw visions of God' (Ezekiel 1:1). His account of what he saw profoundly impresses readers to this day, the overriding impressions being of the majesty and the holiness of the Almighty. Is this not a vital element in the work of the Spirit today?

When Jesus first met Nathanael, he said to him, 'Very truly I tell you, you will see "heaven open, and the angels of God ascending and descending on" the Son of Man' (John 1:51). This predicted the revelation that Nathanael would receive of the transcended Jesus. Is this not what the Spirit purposes to do for each of Jesus' disciples?

Stephen, when about to suffer a cruel martyr's death, declared, 'Look . . . I see heaven open and the Son of Man standing at the right hand of God' (Acts 7:56). Whether it be by walking daily with the Master on the way of the cross, or on the road to martyrdom, the dove-like Holy Spirit's ministry is to reveal to every pilgrim the majesty and strength of the ascended Christ.

Three chapters further on in Acts, we read that Peter 'saw heaven opened and something like a large sheet being let down to earth by its four corners' (Acts 10:11). The rest of the story tells us that what Peter saw opened his understanding to, and acceptance of, the truth that 'God does not show favouritism but accepts from every nation the one who fears him and does what is right' (vv. 34-35). This revelation from an open heaven came as a bombshell to Peter, and later to the remainder of the infant Church. The gospel message of peace with God through Jesus Christ was for Jews and non-Jews, equally. Throughout subsequent centuries, and to the contemporary Church, the Holy Spirit has been speaking along the same lines from an open heaven, urging Christians to communicate the grace of God to all, without exception. How hard it seems to be for us to keep this always in mind and to put it into practise. Charles Wesley's words can help us: 'For all, for all my Saviour died'.[21]

From beginning to end, the book of Revelation is an account of what the apostle John saw and heard when heaven was opened to him. Let us remind ourselves of two instances in particular. In chapter 4:1, John writes: 'I looked, and there before me was a door standing open in heaven.' A voice invited John to 'Come up here', and he did, to see wonders beyond the capacity of human language to fully explain. Surely it is right to insist that heaven is open today, and that the Spirit is calling us to look and to receive understanding and revelation of him who sits on heaven's throne. Further on, in verse 11 of chapter 19, John records: 'I saw heaven standing open and there

---

21. Charles Wesley, 1707-88, 'Let Earth and Heaven Agree', https://hymnary.org/text/let_earth_and_heaven_agree_angels_and (accessed 8.8.23).

before me was a white horse, whose rider is called Faithful and True.' This revelation is of Jesus Christ, the Warrior-King who will come to wage war on his and our enemies, in order to establish his end-time reign, in preparation for the great and final divine act of judgement which will precede the replacement of the present heaven and earth by a new heaven, a new earth and a new Jerusalem. What a momentous revelation! Impossible, then, to not believe that the dove-like Spirit is inviting all who love Jesus, and his appearing, to see into heaven and to be amazed, as John Baptist was at Jesus' baptism, and as the apostle John was when he, on his island prison, looked up, entered in, and saw.

'He saw the Spirit of God'

In his first letter to Timothy, Paul wrote that God is invisible (1 Timothy 1:17); John 1:18 says, 'No one has ever seen God'. These statements fit perfectly with our personal experiences. Nevertheless, God, though immortal and invisible has, in his wisdom and love, acted to make himself visible to men in many ways, most importantly by the incarnation of God the Son as the Son of Man. The blessed third person of the Godhead has taken on various forms to reveal himself to humanity, and presently it is the dove form that we are considering. When John saw the dove he saw God, God the Holy Spirit. The tenor of the account seems to indicate the dove was very real, a divine manifestation. And the statement is clear; in seeing the dove 'he saw the Spirit of God'.

'Descending like a dove'

In common with many other birds, but not all, the dove descends gently, without fracas, and with precision. Being a creature of the skies, the dove must always descend to alight. Numerous Bible texts which, very pointedly, describe the giving of the Spirit as a coming down or a pouring out; in normal circumstances, on earth, nothing comes upwards or pours upwards! The eternal habitat of the Spirit is heaven; he comes down, dove-like, to bring heaven to earth, to bring that which is above humankind here below . . . to bring meekness, purity, peace, comfort and companionship to believers, that they might become more Christ-like.

'And alighting on him'

This phrase asks us to close our eyes and visualise the scene; the dove descending gently and alighting on Jesus . . . his head or his shoulder? We don't know, but we have the impression that the dove remained visibly on him for some time. Nevertheless, the visibility of the dove did come to an end, but the abiding presence of the Spirit did not; the Spirit abode; he remained. Isaiah's messianic prophecies spring to mind: 'The Spirit of the LORD will rest on him – the Spirit of wisdom and of understanding' (11:2); and in 42:1 the Father speaks of 'my servant . . . I will put my Spirit on him'.

Jesus left the Jordan to return to Nazareth, and there he was able to declare, and oh, how true it was:

The Spirit of the Lord is on me, because he has anointed me to proclaim good news to the poor. He

has sent me to proclaim freedom for the prisoners and recovery of sight for the blind, to set the oppressed free, to proclaim the year of the Lord's favour.
(Luke 4:18-19)

Anointing is another scriptural metaphor for the empowering by the Holy Spirit. Generally, the image is that of anointing with oil, but at the river it was a dove that came down on the Messiah. Yes, the Spirit's coming down was to accord power and authority, but these would often be exercised by the Man of Galilee with dove-like gentleness and meekness.

Since they were written, and no doubt during the earlier period when they were only in oral form, Christians have found the accounts of Jesus' baptism deeply moving, and this for several reasons, one being that the presence and unity of the three persons of the Godhead are clearly and beautifully in evidence. The sinless Son, in obedience to the Father, identifies with fallen but repentant humans in asking for, and insisting on, baptism; by an anointing of lowliness and power, the Spirit opens the door for the newly baptised Son to step out and begin his public ministry, after first leading him into the desert in order to be subjected to forty days of temptation and combat with Satan from which he came out victorious; the Father expresses the delight he has in his Son, and from heaven says, 'This is my Son, whom I love; with him I am well pleased' (Matthew 3:17). We read this with open hearts and minds and the dove-like Spirit speaks to us, imprints the truth on our hearts and inspires us to worship; we might use Harriet Auber's words:

O praise the Father, praise the Son
Blest Spirit praise to Thee;
all praise to God, the Three in One,
The One in Three.[22]

Now for a big step back in history to join Noah in the ark, no longer afloat on the mighty flood but aground somewhere on the mountains of Ararat, for the water level had begun to fall. Noah needed clearer and more precise information regarding the location and altitude of the grounded vessel. So, Genesis 8:6-11 tells us:

After forty days Noah opened a window he had made in the ark and sent out a raven, and it kept flying back and forth until the water had dried up from the earth. Then he sent out a dove to see if the water had receded from the surface of the ground. But the dove could find nowhere to perch because there was water over all the surface of the earth; so it returned to Noah in the ark. He reached out his hand and took the dove and brought it back to himself in the ark. He waited seven more days and again sent out the dove from the ark. When the dove returned to him in the evening, there in its beak was a freshly plucked olive leaf! Then Noah knew that the water had receded from the earth.

What a delightful picture of mutual confidence and faithfulness, between Noah and his dove, and of the dove as a messenger of assurance, certainty and peace.

---

22. Harriet Auber, 1773-1862, 'Our Blest Redeemer', https://hymnary.org/text/our_blest_redeemer_ere_he_breathed (accessed 8.8.23).

The dove-like Spirit brings all of these gifts to believers:

> . . . those who are led by the Spirit of God are the children of God. The Spirit you received does not make you slaves, so that you live in fear again; rather, the Spirit you received brought about your adoption to sonship. And by him we cry, 'Abba, Father.' The Spirit himself testifies with our spirit that we are God's children.
> *(Romans 8:14-16)*

During the First World War, members of the dove family became renowned for their exploits in carrying messages from partisans deep in German-held territory to waiting commanders on the allied-controlled side. Today, as in the past, Christians live and witness in territory under the partial control of 'the ruler of the kingdom of the air' (Ephesians 2:2). The Holy Spirit constantly keeps us informed and encouraged by the messages from heaven he conveys to us.

We are indebted to Luke, and to the Spirit, for the inclusion in the third Gospel of the story of the important, but often overlooked, act that Mary and Joseph accomplished forty days after Jesus' birth.

> When the time came for the purification rites required by the Law of Moses, Joseph and Mary took him to Jerusalem to present him to the Lord (as it is written in the Law of the Lord, 'Every firstborn male is to be consecrated to the Lord'), and to offer a sacrifice in keeping with what is said in the Law of the Lord: 'a pair of doves or two young pigeons'.
> *(Luke 2:22-24)*

The Law stipulated that the preferred choice of offering was a lamb and a pigeon or a dove, but poor parents could bring an alternative, and that was the offering brought by Joseph and Mary. On that day, Jesus, his mother, and Joseph were associated with the poor and lowly of our world. Furthermore, since the Holy Spirit is dove-like, he too on that day, as always, willingly associated with the poor and the humble, more particularly with those who are poor and meek in spirit (Matthew 5:3).

The inclusion of the dove among the animals offered in sacrifice suggests a further line of thought. Jesus was and is one with the Spirit, as he was and is one with the Father, and this must imply that when Jesus suffered, in life and in dying, the Holy Spirit suffered too. When Jesus offered himself as a sacrifice for the poor, that is the spiritually impoverished, was not the dove-like Spirit suffering as well? 2 Corinthians 5:19: 'God was in Christ, reconciling the world unto himself' (KJV).

When he attended the synagogue service in Nazareth, not long after leaving the Jordan, Jesus plainly and authoritatively declared that the descent on him of the Spirit was an anointing of power (Luke 4:18-19 and chapter 4 of this book). But the dove-like nature of the anointing remained, for the Galilean was to exercise authority and power in such a meek, lowly, innocent, gracious and peaceable manner that it would ever be true that the dove-like Spirit remained on him. The dove disappeared but the Spirit abode.

By the new birth, by the baptism by the Spirit and by his continuous sanctifying influence, the Holy Spirit imparts to believers the many and varied facets of his character and way of working; on the one hand he is like fire, streams of living water, new wine and much else, and on the other he is gentle, meek and harmless as a dove. Furthermore, the divine plan for Christians is that they become more and more dove-like in beauty; this goes for Christians individually and collectively, i.e. the Church, the bride of Christ. 'Even while you sleep among the sheepfolds, the wings of my dove are sheathed with silver, its feathers with shining gold' (Psalm 68:13). Do we hear the bridegroom, the Christ, saying of his bride, the Church, 'my dove, my perfect one, is unique' (Song of Songs 6:9).

The first draft of this 'dove' text was written while my wife and I were holidaying, with one of our granddaughters, in a comfortable second floor *gîte* in the French Jura mountain range. A few days after our arrival, we noticed a relief painting hanging in the stairwell; central to the picture was a dove in full flight, with a sunrise, or sunset, backdrop. The colours were vivid and attractive, the painting was there for all to see; we had passed it by several times, but for some days we simply hadn't noticed it. Was this symbolic of our often not noticing the presence, the beauty and the actions of the Spirit?

Roy Hession's little book *The Calvary Road*[23] communicates a very big challenge to its readers. We offer the following extract as a conclusion to our reflections on the dove-like Spirit.

The Dove and the Lamb.

Victorious living and effective soul winning service are not the product of our better selves and hard endeavours, but are simply the fruit of the Holy Spirit.

---

23. Roy Hession, *The Calvary Road* (Fort Washington, PA: Christian Literature Crusade, 1950), pp. 32-33.

We are not called upon to produce the fruit, but simply to bear it. . . . [Therefore] we should be continuously filled with the Holy Spirit, or to keep to the metaphor, that the 'trees of the Lord should be continuously full of sap' – His sap.

How this may be so is graphically illustrated by the record, in the first chapter of John, of how the Holy Spirit came upon the Lord Jesus at His baptism. John the Baptist had seen Jesus coming to him and had said of Him, 'Behold the Lamb of God, which taketh away the sin of the world.' Then as he baptised Him, he saw the heavens opened and the Spirit of God descending like a Dove and lighting upon Him.

The Humility of God.

What a suggestive picture we have here – the Dove descending upon the Lamb and resting upon Him! . . . The lamb speaks of meekness and submissiveness and the dove speaks of peace (what is more peaceful than the cooing of a dove on a summer day). Surely this shows us that the heart of Deity is humility. When the eternal God chose to reveal Himself in His Son, He gave Him the name of the Lamb; and when it was necessary for the Holy Spirit to come into the world, He was revealed under the emblem of the Dove. Is it not obvious, then, that the reason why we have to be humble in order to walk with God is not merely because God is so big and we are so little, that humility befits such little creatures – but because God is so humble?[24]

---

24. Hession, *The Calvary Road*, p. 35.

Further on he writes: 'when we have been willing to humble ourselves, as the Lord humbled himself, the Dove will return to us.'[25]

Return, O holy Dove, return,
Sweet messenger of rest;
I hate the sins that made
Thee mourn,
and drove Thee from my breast.[26]

Jonah

This Old Testament prophet's name signifies 'dove' but, excepting the period which began with him asking to be thrown into the sea, followed by the three days inside the great fish and concluded by his going to Nineveh, he had great difficulty being dove-like in his thinking and acting. Before this period, he displayed unfaithfulness, heading off westward to Tarshish instead of eastward to Nineveh, and, after that period of restoration and subsequent effective ministry in Nineveh, he got very angry and greatly displeased when he realised that the Lord had decided to have compassion on the repentant Ninevites.

It follows that Christians endeavouring to implement the mandate Jesus gave to all his disciples (Matthew 28:19-20) must be like lambs among the 'Ninevites' of their day; only as lambs can Jesus' messengers know the abiding endowment of the dove-like Spirit.

---

25. Ibid., p. 36.
26. William Cowper, 1731-1800, 'Walking With God', https://hymnary.org/text/o_for_a_closer_walk_with_god (accessed 8.8.23).

Notes concerning doves

It is commonly understood in politics and diplomacy, a 'dove' is a person who advocates peaceful and conciliatory policies, especially in foreign affairs. Compare it with 'hawk'.

Comparisons, we often say, are odious, and they are sometimes quite unfair; it is not our intention to be derogatory regarding other species of our feathered friends, but the following (likely inspired by something I read, but here rendered in my own words) may help us to more fully appreciate the dove family and, more importantly, to easily assimilate some of the beautiful attributes of the Holy Spirit:

- The dove does not carry a detached, unapproachable air as does the golden eagle; rather, she has an air of simplicity, and she appreciates the company of humans.

- She is not proud in appearance as is the swan; rather, she is of humble disposition.

- She is not big and of impressive wingspan as is the albatross; rather, she is small and does not attract attention because of her size.

- She is not a bird of prey as is the falcon; she is not aggressive, but rather inoffensive with regard to other creatures.

- She is neither a thief as is the magpie, nor deceitful and lazy as the cuckoo appears to us to be; rather, she respects the nests of others and works for her family.

- She does not cry out loudly as does the cock; rather, her voice is soft and lilting.

- She is not considered to be of great (monetary) value as the peacock may be; as we have noted she was the sacrificial offering of the poor.

Andrew Reed wrote of the Spirit:

Come as the dove, and spread your wings,
The wings of peaceful love;
And let your Church on earth become
Blest as Thy Church above.[27]

---

27. Andrew Reed, 1787-1862, 'Spirit Divine, Attend Our Prayers', https://hymnary.org/text/spirit_divine_attend_our_prayers (accessed 8.8.23).

4

Oil

Industrial scale exploitation of mineral oils began in Pennsylvania in the mid-nineteenth century. Since then, the world, and virtually all its inhabitants, have become ever more dependent on this amazing carbon-based matter found in the earth's crust. The nations have become increasingly anxious and self-protective regarding the accessibility of mineral oils, their availability in the world marketplace, their cost and the constantly widening field of uses to which they are being put. Today, mineral oil-based products are used in virtually all areas of human activity, particularly energy production, transport and the manufacture of a vast and varied range of petrochemical and agrochemical products which either enrich or impoverish our lives. When we reflect on how well, or badly, humanity is accomplishing the role God has conferred on them to manage and protect the earth's environment and ecological systems, we automatically give particular attention (pluses and minuses) to the manner in which we use mineral oils.

Long before mineral oils attained their dominant place in world and household economics, humanity was very successfully using vegetable and animal oils in many of life's essential and non-essential activities, including culinary purposes, soothing and healing sores and other ills, lighting and heating, lubrication, cosmetics and religious rites.

Our present interest in oil as a metaphor for the Holy Spirit concerns only vegetable oils, almost exclusively olive oil. Nevertheless, before forgetting our introductory notes concerning mineral oils and their derivatives, and recognising the important place they have in our common mindset, we can assert that just as these oils are currently so highly valued and appreciated, so our Christian mindset should be centred upon Jesus, of course, but also on the Spirit, for in him there is boundless energy and power, and there are uncountable areas of living which he longs to enrich. Furthermore, the worldwide impact and importance of mineral oils remind us that God the Holy Spirit is all-powerful and everywhere present, and that the day is coming when this will be evident to all: 'In the last days, God says, I will pour out my Spirit on all people' (Acts 2:17).

The olive tree is evergreen, small, not particularly attractive, but generally very productive. Its fruit is also small, of oval shape, green, turning to bluish-black when ripe. Oil is extracted from the fruit by beating, treading or, more commonly nowadays, by crushing in a purpose-designed mill. In principle, usage of this oil has not changed much since Bible days; culinary, cosmetic, healing, lighting and religious usage are still, as then, present, in varying degrees, in many cultures. Today, in the world's more affluent areas, where cardiovascular disease is widespread, much is made of the cholesterol-reducing capacity of olive oil used in spreads and cooking. We may doubt that the people of the Mediterranean Basin, in Moses' day, possessed this knowledge! Maybe at that time the known health-giving effects of this oil were limited to its use externally as an ointment or embrocation; we now understand that its consumption is health beneficial; that's progress!

An NIV Study Bible note on James 5:14 informs us that oil was one of the best-known ancient medicines and was mentioned by Philo, Pliny and the physician Galen in their writings.[28] The use of oil, predominantly olive oil, in Israelite and Jewish culture, and religious ritual, is clearly and fully explained in the Old Testament; these usages are referred to metaphorically in both Testaments in order to convey and elucidate spiritual truths.

It is interesting to note that the land promised to the Israelites as a new home, after their wilderness wanderings, was not only 'flowing with milk and honey' (Exodus 3:8) for, together with other bountiful produce, it had a plentiful supply of olive oil (Deuteronomy 8v8). Clearly God had foreseen and provided for his people's household and religious needs.

Anointing

Of all the usages of oil mentioned in the Bible, there is only one which is clearly referred to as a figure of the Holy Spirit and his works, and that is anointing. Nevertheless, this strong metaphoric link of anointing oil to the Spirit tends to give Bible readers the impression that they can freely accord a figurative application when other uses of oil are

---

28. Paraphrased from NIV Study Bible (London: Hodder & Stoughton, 1987), p. 1845.

mentioned. In many cases this seems to be reasonable, and edifying, but care must be taken to avoid building doctrine on this basis.

The Old Testament tells us a lot about anointing oil, and our research starts in Genesis, the book of beginnings. In the twenty-eighth chapter we read the amazing, and easy to visualise, story of the dream Jacob had during an overnight open-air stop. When he awoke early next morning, in gratitude and acceptance of what the Lord had said to him in the dream, Jacob 'took the stone he had placed under his head and set it up as a pillar and poured oil on top of it' (v. 18). He also made a consecration vow to God and renamed the location 'Bethel' A little further on, in Genesis 31:13, we learn that God regarded the pouring on of oil as an anointing: 'I am the God of Bethel, where you anointed a pillar and where you made a vow to me.' Anointing with oil may or may not have been a widespread practice at the time. But the Scriptures make it clear that in subsequent years God accorded a major role to the practice in Israelite culture.

In order to clearly establish the metaphoric link between anointing with oil and the anointing of the Holy Spirit, we now take an approximately 1,200-year leap forward[29] from Jacob to look at a prophecy delivered by Isaiah, in chapter 61:1-3:

The Spirit of the Sovereign LORD is on me, because *the LORD has anointed me* to proclaim good news to the poor. He has sent me to bind up the broken-hearted, to proclaim freedom for the captives and release from darkness for the prisoners, to proclaim

---

29.   NIV Study Bible, Chart on Old Testament Chronology, page not numbered.

the year of the LORD's favour and the day of vengeance
of our God . . .
(my emphasis)

The immediate context and application were probably
the restoration of Zion after the return of the Jewish
remnant from exile in Babylon, and it could be that, in
the first instance, the 'me' in verse 1 was Isaiah himself.
Subsequently, the text was probably understood in a
messianic sense by most Jews, but, most importantly, Jesus
said, quite wonderfully, that it applied to him.

Shortly after his baptism in the river Jordan, and the
descent upon him of the Holy Spirit in the form of a dove,
Jesus visited the synagogue in Nazareth; there he read
Isaiah's prophecy and declared that it was fulfilled in
himself (Luke 4:16-21); he thereby proclaimed that he was
the anointed one, the Messiah (Hebrew: *Masiah)*, or the
Christ (Greek: *Christos*). The Hebrew and Greek words are
both rooted in the notion 'to smear with oil'. The oil of the
Spirit was upon him, and this was manifest in all that he
was, said and did.

During the early years of gospel propagation, Peter
enthusiastically said to a non-Jewish audience (this was a
new experience for him):

You know what has happened throughout the province
of Judea, beginning in Galilee after the baptism that
John preached – how God *anointed* Jesus of Nazareth
with the Holy Spirit and power, and how he went
around doing good and healing all who were under
the power of the devil, because God was with him.
(Acts 10:37-38, my emphasis)

Matthew has left us a similar record in his Gospel where, in chapter 11:5, he reports Jesus' message to John Baptist, who was then in prison and in need of reassurance, 'The blind receive sight, the lame walk, those who have leprosy are cleansed, the deaf hear, the dead are raised, and the good news is proclaimed to the poor.'

The songster Sons of Korah must have been a very gladsome band, going by Psalm 45, a messianic statement which they composed; part of it is quoted in the letter to the Hebrews, speaking of God the Son, 'Your throne, O God, will last for ever and ever; a sceptre of justice will be the sceptre of your kingdom. You have loved righteousness and hated wickedness; therefore God, your God, has set you above your companions by *anointing you with the oil of joy*' (Hebrews 1:8-9, my emphasis). What wonderful company the Son of Man must have been! Despite the heavy burden he carried, his companions benefited, day after day, from the immense gladness and joy which emanated from his person. We are his companions too! For Jesus Holy Spirit anointing was a very gladsome and joyful reality.

But this did not spare the Anointed One from the anger, the plotting and the violent opposition of humanity in general and rulers in particular. Being so different from everyone else, so compassionate, so loving, so truthful and so severe concerning all evil-doing, in short so anointed and set apart, drew to him, and to his followers after Pentecost, the rage of 'the nations', initially the leaders of the Jews, whose wrath culminated in the crucifixion, and countless persons thereafter. The persecuted early believers cited Psalm 2 in their prayer recorded in Acts 4:25-26: 'Why do the nations rage and the peoples plot in vain? The kings of the earth rise up and the rulers band together against the Lord and against his *anointed one'* (my emphasis) Today, as this text is being written, many suffering Christians worldwide, twenty-first century representatives of the *Anointed One*, are probably praying in the same manner.

Let us now return to the Old Testament in order to take note of how the gap we left when we jumped from Genesis 28 and 31 to Isaiah 61, and also the period from Isaiah to the beginning of Jesus' ministry, which were times of divine revelation concerning anointing, associated with the establishment of important customs and practices in Israelite culture. The forty-year long period of Israel's wilderness wanderings, which followed the exodus from Egypt, was very rich in divine revelation concerning God's plan for the social, family and community religious life of the people and the nation. The commandments, promises, social and religious structures, rites and rituals, communicated by God to Moses, who in turn transmitted all to the people, constituted a detailed and binding covenant between Yahweh, the Creator-deliverer, and his chosen redeemed people, Israel. Much in this covenant, more probably everything, foretold and came to fulfilment in the New Covenant established by Jesus Christ.

With this principle in mind, we can take note of the several anointing practices established in the revelations which Moses received from Yahweh concerning the Tabernacle, its furnishings and the priesthood, together with the further similar practices which came into being in later years, all of which prefigured the much greater and altogether perfect Holy Spirit anointings which are such an essential part of the New Covenant.

God instructed Moses to anoint with a sacred oil the persons and objects central to the religious system he, through Moses, put in place as part of the Sinaitic Covenant. These were: 1) Aaron, Moses' brother, and his sons, together with their priestly clothes, as part of their ordination into the priesthood; for Aaron it was to the high priesthood; this anointing enshrined the notions of divine recognition, consecration, setting apart 'for all generations to come' (Leviticus 6:18) and endowment of authority; 2) the altar of burnt offering; here, in addition to consecration, the purpose of the anointing was to purify and make holy; 3) the Tabernacle, or Tent of Meeting, and its furnishings, including the ark of the Testimony, the table on which the bread of the Presence was placed, the lampstand and the altar of incense; these were consecrated by anointing in order to be 'most holy' (Exodus 29:37); 4) the laver, or washbasin, and its stand; this was located between the tent and the altar; it had a humble function, for it was here that Moses and the priests washed their hands and feet; the lowly basin was anointed and consecrated. Here are a few passages in the book of Exodus which tell the story of these anointings:

- Exodus 28:41: 'After you put these clothes on your brother *Aaron and his sons*, anoint and ordain them. Consecrate them so they may serve me as priests' (my emphasis).

- Exodus 29:36-37: 'Purify *the altar* [of burnt offering] by making atonement for it, and anoint it to consecrate it. For seven days make atonement for the altar and consecrate it. Then the altar will be most holy, and whatever touches it will be holy' (my emphasis).

- Exodus 30:26-29: 'Then use it [the sacred anointing oil] to anoint *the tent of meeting, the ark of the covenant law, the table and all its articles, the lampstand and its accessories, the altar of incense, the altar of burnt offering and all its utensils, and the basin with its stand. You shall consecrate them so they will be most holy, and whatever touches them will be holy'* (my emphasis).

- Exodus 29:7: clearly explains that anointing did not mean letting a few drops of the sacred oil fall on a person's head, for it says, 'Take the anointing oil and anoint him [Aaron] by *pouring* it on his head' (my emphasis).

- Psalm 133 provides a fuller and very vivid picture by comparing brotherly unity to the *'precious oil poured on the head*, running down on the beard, running down on Aaron's beard, down on the collar of his robe' (v. 2, my emphasis). What a graphic, comic and surprising sight that must have been. God was not sparing in his ways with his priests; rather, he was extravagant!

Many years later, God acceded to Israel's demands and gave them kings. These were set apart and inducted into office by anointing. Saul was the first, 1 Samuel 9:16 and 10:1, then came David:

The Lord said to Samuel . . . *Fill your horn with oil* and be on your way; I am sending you to Jesse of Bethlehem. I have chosen one of his sons to be king . . . Samuel took the horn of oil and anointed him [David] in the presence of his brothers, and from that day on the Spirit of the Lord came powerfully upon David.
(1 Samuel 16:1,13, my emphasis)

Solomon, the next in line, was anointed by Zadok the priest and Nathan the prophet (1 Kings 1:34-39). On occasions it also became the practice to anoint prophets into office; 1 Kings 19:16 records the Lord's instruction to Elijah to anoint Elisha to succeed him as prophet.

'God anointed Jesus of Nazareth'

This simple but elegant statement by Peter (Acts 10:38) aptly resumes the greatness, and the importance, of what the Father did for the Son prior to the commencement of his earthly ministry. To more fully understand the anointing Jesus received, and which remained an untarnished reality for the remainder of his days on earth, it is helpful to see in the Tabernacle, and all things associated with it, together with the Aaronic priesthood, prefigures of the person and the works our Lord Jesus Christ. On this basis we can build a comprehensive picture of how the various anointings bestowed on objects and persons under the Mosaic Covenant are types of the Holy Spirit anointing poured out upon the Son by God the Father. We must also take into account the additional and later practice of anointing kings and prophets. Taken together these practices give us a grand overall understanding of Jesus:

- He was the anointed *prophet, priest and king* par excellence; he was and is perfect in consecration, holiness and justice; furthermore, the persecuted early Christians recognised in their prayer to God, their Sovereign Lord, that Jesus was the *'holy servant'* whom he had anointed (Acts 4:27, my emphasis);

- He was the anointed one, the Christ, the Messiah who *tabernacled*, pitched his tent, 'made his dwelling' among us (John 1:14);

- The place where he offered himself for sin, in order to appease his Father's wrath, was sanctified or made holy; Calvary was not a pretty place, and the crosses erected there were instruments of brutal, cruel death; all persons executed by crucifixion suffered dreadfully, but none as much as the Christ, for he bore the full force of his Father's wrath incurred by humanity's sin; it is amazing to note that, just like the altar of burnt offering, Calvary and the *ghastly cross* to which Messiah was nailed can be considered to have been anointed by the Spirit, set apart and made holy;

- The Spirit's anointing was upon every aspect of Jesus' ministry when he was on earth, and continues now that he is in heaven; the *ark of the Testimony* (or the covenant) symbolised God's throne and his presence among his people (thus prefiguring Immanuel, God with us – Isaiah 7:14; Matthew 1:23); the ark contained the *stone slabs* on which were written the Ten Commandments (representative of God's Word, and Jesus who was to be the Word made flesh), a quantity of *manna* (symbolic of God's *daily providential caring* for his people, and pointing forward to Jesus, the *bread of life* – John 6:35) and *Aaron's rod that miraculously budded*, blossomed and produced almonds (see Numbers 17 – by this act God publicly confirmed and vindicated his choice of Aaron as high priest, and this prefigured his later affirmation that his

Son had, in the words of Hebrews 7:16-17 (my emphasis), 'become a priest not on the basis of a regulation as to his ancestry but on the basis of the power of an indestructible life . . . *a priest for ever*'; an anointed priesthood); a *gold cover*, the 'mercy seat', was made for the ark, and it was here that the high priest effected an act of atonement, or reconciliation, for the nation (this was by means of sprinkling the shed blood of animals on the cover, and Jesus' blood, shed once for all time, 'is the atoning sacrifice for our sins, and not only for ours but also for the sins of the whole world' – 1 John 2:2); an anointed *place of mercy*;

- The *table* on which was 'put the bread of the presence', which was to be before the Lord 'at all times' (Exodus 25:30); the twelve loaves helped the twelve tribes of Israel to acknowledge the unfailing goodness and anointed presence of Yahweh – New Covenant believers readily understand this as a type of Christ who is ever with them;

- The anointed *lampstand*, with its accessories, is also an obvious prefigure of Jesus, the 'light of the world' (John 8:12);

- The *altar* on which *incense was burnt*, symbol of the prayers of priests and people, was anointed in order that it might be 'most holy' to the Lord (Exodus 40:10); the Son of Man, Jesus the Anointed One, was and is most holy; his recorded prayers, particularly that of John 17, reflect the power and the purity of the Holy Spirit anointing that rested upon him;

- When considering the *laver, or washbasin*, our imagination flies to the staggering and astonishing act of love and service that Jesus carried out for his disciples in the upper room; he washed their feet (John 13:1-17);

- Before entering the Tabernacle in order to carry out their functions, the Old Covenant priests had to wash hands and feet at the humble, but anointed, washbasin; New Covenant priests, that is, all believers, God's present-day servants, must constantly come to their *lowly but anointed Lord*, for cleansing (1 John 2:1-2)

The sacred anointing oil

The Lord instructed Moses concerning the ingredients, and the skills, to be used in the making of the anointing oil. He said:

> Take the following fine spices: 500 shekels of liquid myrrh, half as much (that is, 250 shekels) of fragrant cinnamon, 250 shekels of fragrant calamus, 500 shekels of cassia – all according to the sanctuary shekel – and a hin [some say about 4 litres] of olive oil. Make these into a sacred anointing oil, a fragrant blend, the work of a perfumer. It will be the sacred anointing oil. *Then use it . . .*
> *(Exodus 30:23-26, my emphasis)*

We note the detail regarding the ingredients which, with the exception of the olive oil, were probably costly and quite rare, the precision regarding the quantities, the harmonious and enchanting character of the finished product (the ingredients blended perfectly and, in olfactory terms, the result was 'fragrant'), much being due to the careful and skilled work of an experienced craftsman. For the Lord, Moses and the priesthood, the product was sacred and holy.

What this teaches us about God the Spirit we leave to our readers' appreciation, but we cannot resist mentioning one glaringly obvious fact. The type, the anointing oil, and the person prefigured, the Spirit, are both said to be holy. The third person of the Trinity is the *Holy* Spirit. Surely the Spirit's greatest joy has been to anoint and make known the Son, Jesus. Because Jesus is anointed, Christians acclaim with the words of the Song of Songs 1:3: 'Pleasing is the fragrance of your perfumes; your name is like perfume poured out.'

The passage which explains the composition of the anointing oil concludes with several prohibited uses and warnings; see Exodus 32:33. These principles also apply regarding the Holy Spirit; neither he, nor his power, are to be bought with money (this was attempted by a certain Simon, Acts 8:18-19), and we cannot believe that he wants us to seek him primarily in order to receive an ecstatic experience.

Today's anointed priests

The priesthood of all believers is biblical and absolutely essential to the fulfilment of God's plan for humanity, for the establishment of his kingdom and the preparation of the Church, the body of Christ, for the return of Jesus, and the subsequent bringing into being of the eternal state – New Jerusalem, New Heaven and New Earth. God's intention for the Church now and in the future is not a hierarchy but a fraternity, in which every member, female and male, is a priest; the New Testament does not envisage a church with a clergy and laity division; clearly God considers all the members of Christ's body to be of equal value, importance and status. There are, of course, different ministries and spiritual gifts, but regarding priesthood, all believers are on the same plane; there is one High Priest, Jesus the Christ, and the rest of us are priests, all on an equal footing. A New Covenant priest is a person redeemed by the blood of the Lamb, consequently born into the priestly family, and in need of a constant anointing of the Holy Spirit.

Here are a few relevant scriptures:

- 'You also, like living stones, are being built into a spiritual house to be *a holy priesthood*, offering spiritual sacrifices acceptable to God through Jesus Christ' (1 Peter 2:5, my emphasis). The persons addressed are *all* the Christians over a wide area of Asia Minor, see 1:1.

- 'To him who loves us and has freed us from our sins by his blood, and has made us to be a kingdom and *priests* to serve his God and Father – to him be glory and power for ever and ever! Amen' (Revelation 1:5-6, my emphasis).

- 'With your blood you purchased for God persons from every tribe and language and people and nation. You have *made them* to be a kingdom and *priests to serve our God*, and they will reign on the earth' (Revelation 5:9-10, my emphasis).

- *'He* [God] *anointed us,* set his seal of ownership (on us, and put his Spirit in our hearts as a deposit, guaranteeing what is to come' (2 Corinthians 1:21-22, my emphasis).

- *'You* [all to whom John wrote] *have an anointing* from the Holy One, and all of you know the truth' (1 John 2:20, my emphasis); 'As for you, *the anointing* you received from him *remains* in you, and you do not need anyone to teach you. But as *his anointing teaches* you about all things and as that anointing is real, not counterfeit—just as it has taught you, remain in him' (v. 27, my emphasis). These encouraging words confirm the teaching and promises conveyed by Jesus on behalf of his Father and recorded by John in chapters 14-16 of his Gospel; the Greek word translated 'anointing' in these verses is *chrisma* which is close to *christos* (anointed), the Christ, and to *christianos* (an anointed person), a Christian; we are on holy ground here. As priests, all believers are called to bring sacrifices to God, to intercede to the Father on behalf of his people and also all the unreached peoples of our world, to receive from God and transmit what they receive to the needy, to bless one another and to exercise authority in Jesus' name; for these ministries, all Christians need the anointing of the Spirit.

Other uses of oil which, figuratively, speak of the Holy Spirit

Humanity, including Israel, has long benefited from the many uses other than anointing to which oil, notably olive oil, can be put. Scripture does not tell us that these uses are to be regarded as metaphors or figures of the Holy Spirit, but the manner in which certain biblical narratives unfold often leads readers to very naturally assume an obvious spiritualising of the text, with the person of the Holy Spirit at the centre.

Combustion and lighting

The oil in the Tent of Meeting's lamps needed to be replenished often, particularly throughout the night; this was one of the duties of the high priest and his sons; top quality, pure oil was required. Our High Priest wants us to shine in and illuminate dark places; he is ever ready to replenish and renew his disciples' lamps, by an infilling of the Spirit. The Lord said to Moses:

Command the Israelites to bring you clear oil of pressed olives for the light so that the lamps may be kept burning. In the tent of meeting, outside the curtain that shields the ark of the covenant law, Aaron and his sons are to keep the lamps burning before the LORD from evening till morning.
(Exodus 27:20-21)

A parallel text in Leviticus, 24:2-4, says: 'The lamps . . . before the LORD must be tended continually.'

Replenishment also has a beneficial effect on the recipient, the lamp that each believer is; David wrote, in Psalm 18:28: 'You, LORD, keep my lamp burning; my God turns my darkness into light.'

Jesus' parable of the ten virgins, in Matthew 25:1-13, is a powerful reminder to all who await the appearing of

Jesus, the bridegroom; during the waiting period, all must constantly ask him to replenish their oil reserve. So, let us sing:

Give me oil in my lamp, keep me burning.
Give me oil in my lamp, I pray.
Give me oil in my lamp, keep me burning.
Keep me burning till the break of day.[30]

There is no shortage in the oil reservoirs of our Lord; this is graphically explained in one of the visions that God gave to his prophet Zechariah. Chapter 4 of the prophet's book records: 'I see a solid gold lampstand with a bowl at the top and seven lamps on it, with seven channels to the lamps. Also there are two olive trees by it, one on the right of the bowl and the other on its left' (vv. 2-3). Zechariah asked: 'What are these two olive trees on the right and the left of the lampstand? . . . What are these two olive branches beside the two gold pipes that pour out golden oil?' (vv. 11-12). The reply came: 'These are the two who are anointed to serve the Lord of all the earth' (v. 14). There may well be other valid interpretations of this vision, but in the context of our present reflection we suggest:

The lampstand with its several lights is the Church, whose calling is to shine and lighten the world's darkness;
The two olive trees are the two leaders of God's people at Jerusalem at the time of the vision, Joshua, the high priest, and Zerubbabel, the governor, both being types, or prefigures, of the Messiah, Jesus the

---

30. Lyricist unknown, https://hymnary.org/text/give_me_oil_in_my_lamp_keep_me_burning (accessed 9.8.23).

Christ. From the trees, and from the Christ, flow an abundant and constant supply of 'golden oil', symbol of the Spirit, which ensures that the lights continue to burn; thereby the lampstand, the Church in the world, continues to accomplish its commission.

Verse 6 gives a resume of God's counsel to his people then, and now: '"Not by might nor by power, but by my Spirit," says the LORD Almighty.'

Oil as an everyday culinary essential

One of the most touching episodes in Elijah's life is related in 1 Kings 17:7-14. It concerns a widow and her son, and the well-nigh famine conditions in which they subsisted. She didn't have enough flour and oil to prepare a minimum last meal for her son and herself, but she heeded Elijah's request to first bake a cake for him for, said the prophet, 'The jar of flour will not be used up and the jug of oil will not run dry until the day the LORD gives rain on the land' (v. 14). And so it was. Is this not a powerfully comforting message for all Christians who are surrounded by spiritual famine, moral bankruptcy, unfriendly opposition or outright persecution? Our God provides, particularly when the going is almost unbearable . . . he continues to furnish the bread of his Word and the consolation of his Spirit.

Oil for trading

Elijah was succeeded by Elisha, a prophet of great faith. The widow of another prophet was faced with the impossible task of settling her late husband's debts; she harangued Elisha with her problem. He asked, 'What do you have in your house?', 'A small jar of olive oil' was the reply (2 Kings 4:2). Elisha said to her, 'Go round and ask all your neighbours for empty jars. Don't ask for just a few. Then go inside and shut the door behind you and your sons. Pour oil into all the jars, and as each is filled, put it to one side' (vv. 3-4). The widow did as she was instructed; she just kept on pouring until all the jars were full of oil. When she was sure that there were no more jars to fill, she informed Elisha; he said, 'Go, sell the oil and pay your debts. You and your sons can live on what is left' (v. 7).

There are certainly several lessons to learn from this story, but staying within our remit, and assuming that it is reasonable to see in the poured out plentiful supply of oil a prefigure of the Holy Spirit, we quote Mrs. C.H. Morris' joyful and faith-filled lines:

Are you looking for the fulness of the blessing of the Lord
In your heart and life to-day?
Claim the promise of your Father, come according to
His word,
in the blessed old-time way.

Bring your empty earthen vessels, clean through Jesus'
precious blood,
Come, ye needy, one and all;
And in human consecration wait before the throne
of God,
Till the Holy Ghost shall fall.

Like the cruse of oil, unfailing is His grace for evermore,
And his love unchanging still;
And according to His promise with the Holy Ghost
and power,
He will every vessel fill.

He will fill your heart to-day to over-flow . . . ing,
As the Lord commandeth you, 'Bring your vessels, not
a few';
he will fill your heart to-day to over-flow . . . ing
With the Holy Ghost and power.[31]

Oil used as a cosmetic

That oil has probably been widely used as a cosmetic for millennia is not surprising, but to suggest that this usage can in some way be understood as a metaphor for a work of the Holy Spirit takes us aback somewhat. What is our attitude to cosmetics? Do we consider their use to be a sure sign of vanity, or an unfulfilled longing for recognition? Or is their discreet use usually motivated by a sense of polite social etiquette, a desire to please others? In Psalm 104 we find a long catalogue of God's gifts and gracious actions, and one of the gifts, is 'oil to make [people's] faces shine' (v. 15). This seems to be saying, 'Humankind, men and women, take a look in the mirror, and if you see a dullish skin, maybe dry and wrinkled too, make use of your Creator's gift, apply some 'oil'!'

We cannot imagine that the disciples' faces, after they were filled with the Holy Spirit on the Day of Pentecost, were dull and uninspiring; no, they shone, and thereby expressed the mighty work that was going on in their hearts, minds and bodies.

The account in Luke 7 of an occasion when Jesus was the invitee at a Pharisee's house tells us that the etiquette of the day required a host to put oil on the head of his guests (v. 46).

---

31. Mrs C.H. Morris, 'Bring Your Vessels, Not a Few', 1862-1929, https://hymnary.org/text/
are_you_longing_for_the_fullness_of_the_(accessed 9.8.23).

When Moses descended from the heights of Sinai his face shone . . . not surprising, for he had spent forty days and nights talking with the Lord (Exodus 34)! He knew that this effect would fade, so not wanting the people to witness either the shining or the fading, he covered his face with a veil; that happened under the Old Covenant, but the writers of the second letter to the Corinthians conclude their third chapter by first referring to this remarkable event, and then by explaining that the glory bestowed upon all New Covenant believers is infinitely more wonderful than that experienced by Moses; they wrote:

But whenever anyone turns to the Lord, the veil is taken away. Now the Lord is the Spirit, and where the Spirit of the Lord is, there is freedom. And we all, who with unveiled faces contemplate the Lord's glory, are being transformed into his image with ever-increasing glory, which comes from the Lord, who is the Spirit.
(vv. 16-18)

At first sight this is speaking of a cosmetic, or surface, effect, but the action of the Spirit is very much more than skin deep! God bestows his glory on his children in order to fill the temple (their entire beings), but we must acknowledge that there is always a beneficial, even beautifying effect on the outside!

Oil as a healing agent

The Samaritan, hero of Jesus' story recounted by Luke in his Gospel (chapter 10) probably travelled as lightly as possible, but it seems that he was careful to ensure that he carried with him the essentials that would be required in an emergency. He had his first-aid kit in his baggage. So, when he came across the badly beaten and half-dead victim of highway robbers, moved by pity, he was able to bandage the man's wounds, 'pouring on oil and wine' (v. 34).

In the earlier comment on James 5:14, it seems probable that in Bible days, oil was widely used for medicinal purposes. Olive oil, maybe a goodly number of other oils, with or without the addition of minerals, herbs or plant extracts, were probably available from apothecaries. No doubt many households were accustomed to making their own ointments, oils and medicines. In the Old Testament, oil as a healing agent is mentioned figuratively; in the first chapter of Isaiah, the prophet declares that Judah's injuries and afflictions are so serious that they are beyond the soothing power of oil.

A familiar phrase in the shepherd psalm (Psalm 23) springs to memory: 'You anoint my head with oil' (Psalm 23:5). Did the writer, David, have in mind the anointing into the office of king he received from Samuel? Or was he recalling what he did for the injured or sick sheep he tended in his youth?

For many years Phillip Keller was a shepherd in East Africa; in his book on Psalm 23 he has a very helpful passage on this verse. He describes the terrible torment that sheep can suffer as a result of attacks by flies and mosquitoes who lay their eggs in the mucous membranes of the animal's nostrils; the eggs rapidly become larvae which seek to enter the sheep's head and brain, causing intense irritation and inflammation. Keller's remedy was to use a composition of linseed oil with certain additives which he applied on the animal's head and around the nose; this created an effective barrier to the insect attacks. The treatment has to be renewed regularly while the danger persists. Without hesitation, Phillip Keller applies his pastoral experience to himself, a Christian. He explains that in order to be protected against succumbing to the irritations and vexations of everyday life he needs a permanent anointing of the Holy Spirit. He writes: 'In Luke 11:13 Christ himself, our Shepherd, presses us to ask for the Holy Spirit, the gift of the Father. It is a logical and legitimate desire for us to receive a daily anointing of the Holy Spirit.'[32] We heartily endorse Keller's counsel; this is surely the route to take in order to know the Lord's healing and keeping power . . . these together equate to divine health, with which multitudes of believers have been blessed down the ages.

In our reflections upon the healing capacity of oil, and the metaphoric significance of this regarding the Holy Spirit, we must give careful attention to the advice sent by James to his scattered readers:

Is anyone among you ill? Let them call the elders of the church to pray over them and anoint them with oil in the name of the Lord. And the prayer offered in faith will make the sick person well; the Lord will raise them up.

(James 5:14-15)

Some consider that James is encouraging the use of oil for medicinal reasons, and that the passage is saying that although healing comes about because of prayer offered in faith, it may also involve a medical contribution. This is undoubtedly often the case. Others sense that oil anointing

---

32. Phillip Keller, *A Shepherd Looks at Psalm 23* (Grand Rapids, MI: Zondervan, Grand Rapids, 2015), p. 104.

is stipulated as something concrete, graspable and an aid to faith. However, this should not lead us to exclude the view that oil, particularly when used for anointing, is symbolic of the Holy Spirit. The Scriptures clearly show that the ministry of God the Holy Spirit, in unity with that of God the Son, includes physical, psychological and spiritual healing. The Spirit uses elders, other ministerial gifts, spiritual gifts (1 Corinthians 12) and the faith of all who believe: 'These signs will accompany those who believe . . . they will place their hands on people who are ill, and they will get well' (Mark 16:17-18).

The soothing, relaxing and healing effect of oils applied to the body, sometimes as an embrocation, reminds us that the Holy Spirit is our Comforter, our Counsellor, who heals our wounds and makes us well. We can go further and proclaim that we are a joyous and festive people, for the Sovereign Lord has bestowed on us 'the oil of joy' (Isaiah 61:3).

5

Water

Water covers the greater part of the surface of our globe, and its importance is not lost on any living creature. Water's chemical formula, H_2O, appears to most of us to be extremely simple, but add to it or deduct from it results in something that cannot support life. Without water, life is impossible. So, water as a metaphor for the Holy Spirit is very appropriate. All that lives has received life from God, God the Holy Spirit.

The Spirit moved upon the surface of the waters of the primitive oceans and gave those waters the capacity to produce and sustain living organisms; Genesis 1:2 reads: 'Now the earth was formless and empty, darkness was over the surface of the deep, and the Spirit of God was hovering over the waters.' Today, as it always has been, the physical, intellectual and moral life of all human beings depends on the triune God, 'For in him we live and move and have our being' (Acts 17:28). But who needs proof of this? Is it not one of those self-evident truths which is essential to our general well-being and peace of mind?

Here we have a bedrock truth, the acceptance of which is a solid foundation for living and being; its rejection produces uncertainty, instability and purposelessness. As Barnabas and Paul reminded their audience in Lystra, in Acts 14:17: 'He [God] has not left himself without testimony: he has shown kindness by giving you rain from heaven and crops in their seasons . . .'

Giving our attention to water as a symbol, our imaginations fly here and there to all manner of sights which have left indelible impressions on our memories. Gushing mountain streams, gently flowing rivers where we learned to swim, the seemingly endless vastness of the oceans, the clever and intricate use of water in man-made fountains, watermills and hydraulic power stations . . . But we all know that the great essential for each of us is having enough water to drink; this water must be of appropriate quality for human consumption; in Pakistan, at the time this is being written, there are vast quantities of flood water covering the Indus River plains, but they are totally unsuitable for drinking; quality and purity, in sufficient quantity, are essential to humanity. It is no surprise that Jesus, when using the figure of water for the person and work of the Spirit, bases his teaching on that which is mandatory for all . . . the drinking of water, water with life-giving qualities.

In the autumn of the last full year of his ministry on earth, Jesus attended the Feast of Tabernacles in Jerusalem. During the final and most important day of the feast, the seventh or the eighth day:

Jesus stood and said in a loud voice, 'Let anyone who is thirsty come to me and drink. Whoever believes in me, as Scripture has said, rivers of living water will flow from within them.' By this he meant the Spirit, whom those who believed in him were later to receive. Up to that time the Spirit had not been given, since Jesus had not yet been glorified.

John 7:37-39

The scripture to which Jesus refers is probably a combination of texts, perhaps Zechariah 14:8: 'On that day living water will flow out from Jerusalem . . . in summer and in winter', with Ezekiel 47:1-12:

The man brought me back to the entrance of the temple, and I saw water coming out from under the threshold of the temple towards the east . . . Fruit trees of all kinds will grow on both banks of the river. Their leaves will not wither, nor will their fruit fail. Every month they will bear fruit, because the water from the sanctuary flows to them. Their fruit will serve for food and their leaves for healing.

Or Joel 3:18: 'A fountain will flow out of the LORD's house and will water the valley of acacias.' Or Isaiah 58:11: 'The LORD will guide you always; he will satisfy your needs in a sun-scorched land and will strengthen your frame. You will be like a well-watered garden, like a spring whose waters never fail.' Or, another possibility, perhaps Jesus had in mind the occasion when Moses, surrounded by a host of thirsty and protesting Israelites at Horeb was instructed by God, to 'Strike the rock, and water will come out of it for the people to drink' (Exodus 17:6).

A common feature in of all these texts is that they are not speaking of sluggish, meandering rivers, even less of still and stagnant waters; rather, they each convey a picture of moving water, of fast-flowing lively streams, or gushing fountains, that have life-giving potential, that are capable of producing and enhancing life.

The Holy Spirit flows in abundance, and in purity, to the spiritually thirsty; to those who, like the woman Jesus met by a well in Samaria, have hitherto never turned to God in their search for satisfaction and worthwhile purpose, and to Christians who thirst for a deeper and a closer walk with God. The flowing Spirit bears, to all who are open to him, the person of Jesus, he who said 'Everyone who drinks this water [from the well] will be thirsty again, but whoever drinks the water I give them will never thirst. Indeed, the water I give them will become in them a spring of water welling up to eternal life' (John 4:13-14). It is evident that the Son and the Spirit are one in purpose, method and intent. It follows that the opportunity is there for each and every one, seeker or committed Christian, to respond to Jesus, simply and sincerely as the woman did, saying 'Sir, give me this water . . .' (v. 15).

The Century Bible commentary on 'If any man thirst . . .' (John 7:37, RV), offers these thoughts:

The language here employed was probably suggested by the libations of water drawn from the Pool of Siloam each morning of the feast (while Isa.xii. 3 was sung)and carried in a golden vessel by a procession of priests who poured it over the altar at the morning sacrifice. If it was discontinued on the eighth day, as seems probable, in token of their having come into 'a land of springs of water,' [in the sequence of events commemorated during the Feast], the proclamation of Jesus in the temple would be none the less impressive as the offer of satisfaction for the soul whose thirst no Jewish ritual could quench.[33]

Isaiah 12:3 declares: 'With joy you will draw water from the wells of salvation.'

On that important day Jesus foretold that, after the Spirit had been given, streams of living water would flow from each believer, but he stipulated a three-fold pre-condition; three musts for the believer – be thirsty, come to him (Jesus), drink. We note that 'streams' is plural, and that 'living' speaks powerfully of the water's quality and potential.

Thirst

In Psalm 42, a Levite explains that in his earlier years he had a fulfilling priestly role in Jerusalem, but for some reason he had been forced to flee to the Hermon mountain range in the north. Even there, or so it seems, he was pursued by his oppressors; furthermore, the people among whom he was now living taunted him: 'Where is your God?' they asked. He was downcast, depressed. He felt like the hunted, panting mountain deer he had probably seen, or heard of, desperately seeking a life-saving stream of water. The Levite wrote: 'As the deer pants for streams of water, so my soul pants for you, my God. My soul thirsts for God, for the living God.' King David wrote similarly, Psalm 63v1, 'You, God, are my God, earnestly I seek you; I thirst for you, my whole being longs for you, in a dry and parched land where there is no water.' It would be unwise to insist that extreme thirst of this kind, accompanied by an acute sense of imminent danger, leading providentially to a hurried

---

33. *The Century Bible*, p. 197.

intake of life-restoring water, followed by a further dash for safety, gives an invariable picture of the manner in which the God-thirsty believer will be led to drink in the Spirit. But it would be equally unwise to leave it aside on the assumption that it is too extreme, too untypical of the ways of God. To have a great thirst for God, for the Holy Spirit, implies a single-mindedness which will probably, almost certainly, set the thirsty person apart in one way or another. The thirsty one becomes conscious of the price that a disciple has to pay.

Come to me

This is what thirsty believers must do, for Jesus alone has a plentiful supply of living water to give. And believers are accustomed to coming to him, their Saviour, Friend and Advocate. Now he invites them to come because they are thirsty, because they long for more of him, more of the Spirit in order that others, among whom they live, work and socialise, might also benefit from the living streams of the Spirit. Jesus is very welcoming of the thirsty, and when they come to him he kindly, but very firmly, prepares them for the drink they so much long for. The preparation will involve cleansing, correction, rectification of motives and lots more, all part of the discipleship process, including walking with the Master on the Calvary Road.

Drink

This sounds so simple, and no doubt it is, especially for those who have spent time sitting at the Master's feet. The thirsty, the humble and well-prepared disciple will quite simply drink. Jesus said no more than that, and neither will we. But drink deeply we must, in order that the streams might flow.

Drinking of the Spirit, just like imbibing water, is not a 'once and that's it finished' experience. We should regard it as a daily necessity and pleasure. The story of the early Christians, in the book of Acts, relates that after their initial baptism in the Holy Spirit they were regularly, quite evidently, full of the Spirit; for example, Acts 4:31: 'After they prayed . . . they were all filled with the Holy Spirit', and Acts 13:52: 'And the disciples were filled with joy and with the Holy Spirit.' These accounts suggest that they often drank the 'water' that Jesus spoke of at that feast in Jerusalem.

The sad line of *The Rime of the Ancient Mariner*, when he was drifting helplessly on a vast and unfriendly ocean, 'Water, water, everywhere, but not a drop to drink',[34] could in our present context be replaced by, 'Water, water, everywhere (God the Holy Spirit is omnipresent), and all who thirst may drink.'

Those who drink of the Spirit are surrounded by fellow believers who will be refreshed and renewed by the streams of living water that flow rapidly in their direction; others who do not yet know the Saviour will also benefit in many ways from their contact with the same life-giving waters, that is waters that contain grace and compassion, truth and cleansing power.

Jerusalem, or Zion, has no rivers or streams; water was, and doubtless still is, brought into the city from outside via an underground conduit.[35] Yet in Psalm 46:4 the writer

---

34. Samuel Taylor Coleridge, 1772-1834, 'The Rime of the Ancient Mariner'. This is actually a popular misquote of the actual Rime.
35. It was Hezekiah, king of Judah, who constructed a tunnel from the Gihon spring outside the city wall to a cistern within the city; see 2 Kings 20:20; 2 Chronicles 32:30.

exalts in proclaiming loud and clear: 'There is a river whose streams make glad the city of God, the holy place where the Most High dwells.' The Church, the Zion of the New Covenant, likewise has no natural rivers, but God has mercifully and graciously provided a mighty river that has entered the city from outside; the Holy Spirit came down from heaven. The river that burst into Jerusalem on the Day of Pentecost magnificently demonstrated what the psalmist's words prefigured. Surely, too, in this dispensation of the Spirit and of grace, the Church, the people of Zion scattered through all the nations, can praise the Giver with these words from Psalm 65:9-10: 'You care for the land and water it; you enrich it abundantly. The streams of God are filled with water to provide the people with corn, for so you have ordained it. You drench its furrows and level its ridges; you soften it with showers and bless its crops.'

Rain and showers

Rain and showers are two further 'water' metaphors we find in our Bibles. Both are also used as figures for truths and realities other than the Spirit, but Isaiah was inspired to articulate a parallel between rain and the outpouring of the Holy Spirit.

God says, 'Now listen . . . I will pour water on the thirsty land, and streams on the dry ground; I will pour out my Spirit on your offspring, and my blessing on your descendants. They will spring up like grass in a meadow, like poplar trees by flowing streams' (Isaiah 44:1-4). In the previous chapter, in verses 18-21, the prophet declares:

Forget the former things; do not dwell on the past. See, I am doing a new thing! Now it springs up; do you not perceive it? I am making a way in the wilderness and streams in the wasteland. The wild animals honour me, the jackals and the owls, because I provide water in the wilderness and streams in the wasteland, to give drink to my people, my chosen, the people I formed for myself that they may proclaim my praise.

It seems to me to be very appropriate that we read these prophetic words in the light of the New Covenant and apply them to our contemporary situations. Christians are God's people, his chosen people, and consequently, while not forgetting the former mighty works of the Spirit among us (gospel propagation, revivals, growth, transformed communities), we should believe God for streams of living water in the spiritual and moral desert of our contemporary world, and particularly on the dry land, the parched and thirsty ground of our present-day churches and assemblies. Do we see the rain clouds forming, do we hear the pitter-patter of the first raindrops, are we trusting God for refreshing showers, and more . . . for outpourings of the Spirit that will cause the dried and shrivelled seeds in the till now hostile, desert-like hearts of a multitude of persons, to burst into life?

Ezekiel prophesied in similar vein, 34:26: 'I will make them and the places surrounding my hill a blessing. I will send down showers in season; there will be showers of blessing.' It is worth reading the wider passage in verses 25-31. Jeremiah too spoke (Jeremiah 5:24) of these same showers, and he also stipulated that God would faithfully provide autumn rains, at the beginning of the growing season, and spring showers, towards its end. These scriptures may suggest the Holy Spirit showers experienced by the early Church and continued in some measure through the rainy season of Church history, which will be concluded under the blessing of the spring rains, which will precede the final harvest: 'In the last days, God says, I will pour out my Spirit on all people' (Acts 2:17).

These lines have been sung in many languages by multitudes of Christians:

'There shall be showers of blessing':
This is the promise of love;
There shall be seasons refreshing,
Sent from the Saviour above.

. . .

'There shall be showers of blessing' –
Precious reviving again;
Over the hills and the valleys,
Sound of abundance of rain.

Show . . . ers of blessing,
Showers of blessing we need;
Mercy drops round us are falling,
But for the showers we plead.[36]

Zechariah 10:1 tells us: 'Ask the LORD for rain in the springtime'.

In Old Testament times God promised to pour his natural rain on his people's lands; however, the fulfilment of his promise was conditional on their obedience and on their fidelity and integrity, and probably on other aspects of their walk with him. We should assume that the same conditions apply under the New Covenant regarding the

---

36. D.W. Whittle, 1840-1901, 'There Shall Be Showers of Blessing', https://hymnary.org/text/there_shall_be_showers_of_blessing_this (accessed 9.8.23). Whittle wrote under the pseudonym El Nathan.

outpouring of the Spirit. Deuteronomy 28:1-14 tells us about the blessings promised to the people on condition that they obeyed God's commands through Moses: 'If you fully *obey* the LORD your God . . . the LORD will open the heavens, the storehouse of his bounty, to send rain on your land in season and to bless all the work of your hands' (my emphasis). Through the prophet Malachi God spoke severely, but graciously, to Israel, calling the people to *fidelity and integrity* in the management of money matters (and it seems right to apply what God said to all areas of living):

'In tithes and offerings. You are under a curse – your whole nation – because you are robbing me. Bring the whole tithe into the storehouse, that there may be food in my house. Test me in this,' says the LORD Almighty, 'and see if I will not throw open the floodgates of heaven and pour out so much blessing that there will not be room enough to store it. I will prevent pests from devouring your crops, and the vines in your fields will not drop their fruit before it is ripe,' says the LORD Almighty. 'Then all the nations will call you blessed, for yours will be a delightful land,' says the LORD Almighty.

(Malachi 3:8b-12)

We too must heed the conditions, in order that the Lord Almighty may open the heavens, 'open the floodgates' in order that the Holy Spirit might make the Church 'a delightful land'.

Do we see rain clouds forming? Do we hear the pitter-patter of Holy Spirit rain falling here and there in various locations around the world . . . or in our own neighbourhood? Such reflections propel our thoughts to God's Old Testament prophet Elijah; the first book of Kings tells us this amazing story. 'Now Elijah . . . said to Ahab [the king], "As the LORD, the God of Israel, lives, whom I serve, there will be neither dew nor rain in the next few years except at my word"' (1 Kings 17:1). Then in 18:1: 'After a long time, in the third year, the word of the LORD came to Elijah: "Go and present yourself to Ahab, and I will send rain on the land."' Further on in the same chapter, after Elijah's momentous encounter with the priests of Baal, we read in verses 41-46:

And Elijah said to Ahab, 'Go, eat and drink, for there is the sound of a heavy rain.' So Ahab went off to eat and drink, but Elijah climbed to the top of Carmel, bent down to the ground and put his face between his knees. 'Go and look toward the sea,' he told his servant. And he went up and looked. 'There is nothing there,' he said. Seven times Elijah said, 'Go back.' The seventh time the servant reported, 'A cloud as small as a man's hand is rising from the sea.' So Elijah said, 'Go and tell Ahab, 'Hitch up your chariot and go down before the rain stops you.'' Meanwhile, the sky grew black with clouds, the wind rose, a heavy rainstorm came on and Ahab rode off to Jezreel. The power of the LORD came on Elijah and, tucking his cloak into his belt, he ran ahead of Ahab all the way to Jezreel.

During the drought, the situation over the region was serious, indeed desperate, and the people suffered; God's gracious declaration that an end to the drought was nigh was conditional; Elijah, by his obedience, fidelity and integrity, satisfied the conditions, and by his earnest, humble intercession he, as it were, partnered with Almighty God in order that the divine promise be accomplished; the Lord opened the floodgates and poured out his rain on the parched lands.

Through the centuries since the ascension of Jesus, there have no doubt been many outpourings of the Holy Spirit, the essentials of which have closely reflected the mighty rainfall experienced by Elijah and Israel. We too would do well to heed the teaching of James, one of Jesus' brothers who also became one of his apostles:

Therefore confess your sins to each other and pray for each other so that you may be healed. The prayer of a righteous person is powerful and effective. Elijah was a human being, even as we are. He prayed earnestly that it would not rain, and it did not rain on the land for three and a half years. Again he prayed, and the heavens gave rain, and the earth produced its crops.
(James 5:16-18)

Of the many groups of Christians who have taken James' exhortation to heart, those living in the parish of Barvas on the Isle of Lewis in the Outer Hebrides, Scotland, in 1949-52 and 60s, can be an inspiration to we of the twenty-first century. An account by Duncan Campbell,[37] a Presbyterian minister and itinerant evangelist, has much to teach us; it tells of the vital preparatory work accomplished by the Holy Spirit in the lives of believers and local churches, followed by powerful outpourings of the Spirit during which many

---

37. www.revival-library.org/revival_histories/evangelical/twentieth_century/hebrides_revival.shtml (accessed 1.9.23).

were brought to conviction of sin, brokenness in coming to realise the enormity of the love of Jesus, gloriously saved and transformed (some were churchgoers, many not); the effect on island society was dramatic; this was revival, and it was durable.

These verses in Isaiah inspired them: 'I will pour water upon him that is thirsty' (Isaiah 44:3, KJV) and: 'Oh that thou wouldest rend the heavens, that thou wouldest come down, that the mountains might flow down at thy presence . . .' (Isaiah 64:1-3, KJV). Two elderly sisters, one being blind, were beautifully used by the Spirit in prayer and in the giving of sound counsel to their minister. 'Give yourself to prayer; to waiting upon God. Get your elders and deacons together and spend at least two nights a week waiting upon God in prayer.'[38] Folk of neighbouring villages became involved. God was moving in churches, meadows and moorland. Under deep conviction people were coming to Jesus.

Campbell summarised his experience of the revival thus:

It takes the supernatural to break the bonds of the natural. You can make a community mission conscious. You can make a community crusade conscious. But only God can make a community God-conscious. Just think about what would happen if God came to any community in power. I believe that day is coming. May God prepare us all for it. Amen.[39]

We strongly recommend readers to consult the fuller and more detailed reports available on internet. Duncan

---

38. www.revival-library.org/revival_histories/evangelical/twentieth_century/hebrides_revival.shtml (accessed 1.9.23).
39. www.revival-library.org/revival_histories/evangelical/twentieth_century/hebrides_revival.shtml (accessed 1.9.23).

Campbell's sermon, 'When Mountains Flowed Down' can be found in various places online[40], and his book about it is *Revival in the Hebrides*.[41]

So, let us 'Be patient . . . until the Lord's coming. See how the farmer waits for the land to yield its valuable crop, patiently waiting for the autumn and spring rains. You too, be patient and stand firm, because the Lord's coming is near' (James 5:7-8).

No doubt there have been many other modern-day awakenings similar to that of the Isle of Lewis, but less well known or hardly known at all in the wider world. Undoubtedly, too, throughout the twenty centuries that separate us from the period of the Acts of the Apostles, many communities of dried-up believers have been led along a path of repentance and earnest prayer to times of refreshing Holy Spirit rain. Indeed, even earlier, after Cyrus allows their return in 538BC,[42] the company of Jews, who had willingly commenced the re-building of the Temple in Jerusalem, had become discouraged due to intense external opposition, and furthermore they had lost their vision and sense of priority. They had stopped work on the Temple and, instead, were concentrating on building their own houses, which they were carrying out to a luxurious standard. The Lord Almighty was displeased with his people, and in order to reprimand them and convict them of the error of their ways he 'withheld their dew [rain in some translations]' (Haggai 1:10). Through Haggai, the prophet, God said to the people: 'I called for a drought on the fields and the mountains, on the grain, the new wine,

---

40. www.revival-library.org/revival_histories/evangelical/twentieth_century/hebrides_revival.shtml (accessed 1.9.23).
41. Duncan Campbell, *Revival in the Hebrides* (Scotts Valley, CA: CreateSpace Independent Publishing Platform, 2016).
42. NIV Study Bible, p. 1372.

the olive oil and everything else the ground produces, on people and livestock, and on all the labour of your hands' (Haggai 1:11). The Lord Almighty called on the people to 'Give careful thought to your ways' (Haggai 1:5,7). The spiritually and morally parched and barren people did just that.

Under the guidance of their temporal and spiritual leaders they showed their fear of the Lord and 'began to work on the house of the LORD Almighty' (Haggai 1:14). When the rebuilding work is completed, the prophets announce God's promised blessings and abundance (Haggai 2:19; see also Joel 3:18).[43]

Years prior to Haggai (some say 200 to 300 years earlier)[44] another prophet, Joel, spoke God's word to a people whose land was plagued by drought and massive locust destruction. Among the several idioms the prophet used to describe the consequence of the degraded moral and spiritual condition to which the nation had descended we read 'the streams of water have dried up' (Joel 1:20). The element essential to continued living, for people and beasts, was absent. Through Joel, God called upon everyone (including priests, farmers and drunkards) to mourn, repent, pray, rend their hearts and return to him, and he promised that, in response to their obedience to this injunction, he would send 'the autumn rains because he is faithful . . . abundant showers, both autumn and spring rains, as before. The threshing-floors will be filled with grain' (Joel 2:23-24). Today there are communities of believers to whom God has spoken in similar terms, who

---

43. Thoughts stimulated by a message on Haggai preached by my Belgian friend Luc Guizzetti. Used with permission.
44. NIV Study Bible dates Joel to ninth century BC (p. 1317) and Haggai's ministry to 520BC (p. 1373).

have returned to the Lord and been blessed by outpourings of the Holy Spirit.

Furthermore, God, through Joel, has given us a water-inspired prediction related to a coming 'Day', the Day of the Lord, when 'all the ravines of Judah will run with water. A fountain will flow out of the LORD's house and will water the valley of acacias' (Joel 3:18). Is this not a word picture of that 'Day', after Jesus has returned to earth (to Jerusalem) to reign (Revelation 22:1-4), and when the fullness of the Holy Spirit will flow in blessing especially in places which, formerly, had been dry and arid?

Dew

Over the centuries, very many Bible lovers have been greatly blessed when understanding the person and work of the Holy Spirit as to be like dew, and its coming down in refreshing grace on needy pastures and hillsides. At first glance this seems to be surprising, for nowhere in Scripture, where reference is made to dew, is this categorically said to be a metaphor for the Spirit. Nevertheless, bearing in mind what the Gospels and Acts teach us, I remember singing a chorus calling God to let the dew of his Spirit fall on us, as it fell on Hermon.

Dew is formed of droplets of water coalescing at night. It is known that dew is more abundant at certain times of the year and at higher altitudes, and that most often it forms during the latter part of the night, that is not long before dawn, when the recipient surfaces are at their coolest.

Dew starts to form when the dew point in the air has been reached, i.e. when moisture begins to form on a surface the surrounding air is said to have reached its dew point. It is also common knowledge that dew is most abundant when the air is calm or still and the sky cloudless.

Early in the morning, after leaving the dry interior of our home, or our tent at high altitude, we find not a multitude of tiny drops but a blanket of moisture covering fields, hillsides, banks of mountain flowers, crops and animals which have spent the night under the stars. All of nature is refreshed, renewed and revived; the pastures are green and the grass luscious. We feel that we understand how the psalmist felt when he wrote: 'How good and pleasant it is when God's people live together in unity! . . . It is as if the dew of Hermon were falling on Mount Zion. For there the LORD bestows his blessing, even life for evermore' (Psalm 133:1,3).

Snow-capped Mount Hermon, located to the north of Galilee, rises from the plains to 2,814m, and was renowned for the abundance of its morning dews. Its slopes no doubt supported, and presumably still do, a varied and healthy ecosystem. Mount Zion's situation was very different; for it is located much further south, in the dry and arid Judean hills; nevertheless, it was, and is, a place blessed by the God of Abraham, Isaac and Jacob. Jerusalem was built there, and it was there that God Almighty revealed himself to humanity, to Jew and non-Jew. But Mount Zion was quite barren, and little or no dew ever fell on its slopes. Never mind, David was inspired to think, and to write . . . when brethren live together in unity, or travel together harmoniously in pilgrimage to Jerusalem, it is as good as if Hermon's dew was falling on his beloved Zion! The effect was similar; unity gave rise to daily refreshing fellowship, to renewal of vision and purpose, and to life-enhancing revival.

Several centuries later the dew of the Spirit fell on the believers gathered as one somewhere near the Temple on Mount Zion. It was the Day of Pentecost . . . they were 'all together in one place' (Acts 2:1), and 'All of them were filled with the Holy Spirit and began to speak in other tongues as the Spirit enabled them' (Acts 2:4). Ever since, seeking, longing, expectant persons have been wonderfully endued and equipped by the dew that still comes down from heaven.

To the extent that our personal situation allows, let us arise early to appreciate the morning 'dew', to feast upon the refreshed pages of God's Word, to ensure that our praises rise to him in the calm and stillness of the early hours, and then to go forth in the renewed strength we have received. We should also be encouraged, and challenged, by the knowledge that the higher we climb during our early morning devotions, the more profuse will be the 'dew' of the Spirit that falls upon us. However, should we be among the many who must devote their first waking hours to small children, to sick or disabled persons, or some other priority, we can rest assured that the coming down of the dew of the Spirit is not limited to any particular moment of day or night. He descends upon us when our receptivity, our dew point, is present.

The absence of dew is symbolic of spiritual and moral barrenness; King David asked for this curse on Gilboa's mountains, which is where Israel was defeated, Saul and Jonathan killed: 'Mountains of Gilboa, may you have neither dew nor rain, may no showers fall on your terraced fields. For there the shield of the mighty was despised' (2 Samuel 1:21). It is also salutary to recall that long before Saul died, God had withdrawn his Spirit from him; the dew was no longer upon Saul.

On the contrary, God surely wants to be for his people today what he promised to be for Israel.

'I will be like the dew to Israel; he will blossom like a lily. Like a cedar of Lebanon, he will send down his roots; his young shoots will grow; His splendour will be like an olive tree, his fragrance like a cedar of Lebanon' (Hosea 14:5-6). It is important to note that this promise of restoration and abundance was conditional on the return of Israel to the Lord their God, for the nation had been unfaithful and adulterous. The nation was called to come back to the Lord with these words: 'Forgive all our sins and receive us graciously, that we may offer the fruit of our lips' (Hosea 14:2). Then, and only then, their Lord would heal them and 'be like the dew' to them (Hosea 14:5).

Life is not always comfortable; sometimes the dew seems to be absent. It is also a truism that we all experience suffering of many kinds. That was Job's lot. One day, suffering and misunderstood though he was, he allowed his imagination to look forward in faith to happier times to come; he said, 'My roots will reach to the water, and the dew will lie all night on my branches. My glory will not fade; the bow will ever be new in my hand' (Job 29:19-20). It is certainly the will of our Father, and of his Son, to bless our lives with the dew of the Spirit, despite the suffering we may currently be experiencing.

It is clear that Scripture teaches that unity between fellow believers is both a prerequisite to the 'dew' falling upon us, and a consequence of the 'dew' coming down. In an expectant attitude, and disposition of oneness, we need to 'Make every effort to keep the unity of the Spirit through the bond of peace' (Ephesians 4:3).

A phrase in Genesis 27:28 is part of the blessing that Isaac pronounced for his son Jacob; we could bless our own children, natural and spiritual, using the same words, 'May God give you of heaven's dew . . .'!

Andrew Reed wrote this prayer addressed to the Holy Spirit:

Come as the dew, and sweetly bless
This consecrated hour;
May barrenness rejoice to own
Thy fertilizing power.[45]

Horatius Bonar left us these words of testimony to sing and live out:

I heard the voice of Jesus say,
'Behold, I freely give
The living water, thirsty one;
stoop down, and drink, and live.'
I came to Jesus, and I drank
of that life-giving stream;
my thirst was quenched, my soul revived,
and now I live in Him.[46]

45. Andrew Reed, 1787-1862, 'Spirit Divine, Attend Our Prayer', hymntime.com/tch/htm/s/p/i/d/spidivat.htm (accessed 1.9.23)
46. Horatius Bonar, 1808-89, 'I Heard the Voice of Jesus Say', https://hymnary.org/text/i_heard_the_voice_of_jesus_say_come_unto (accessed 9.8.23).

6

New Wine

Jesus' contemporaries said of him that he was 'a glutton and a drunkard' (Matthew 11:19); the KJV translation is even stronger, 'a man gluttonous, and a winebibber'. Such accusations were certainly untrue, but the remainder of what his accusers said was 100 per cent true, for they declared that he was 'a friend of tax collectors and sinners'; he certainly was and still is. Overall, Jesus was probably not unhappy with his adversaries' assessment of his character. Numerous incidents related in the Gospels reveal a Man who enjoyed socialising and sharing a meal, and very often, for it was customary in his day, this would have been accompanied by a glass (or another equally appropriate receptacle) of wine. It was always a memorable occasion!

In the mid-1970s I regularly visited Amsterdam concerning the refurbishment of a city centre property. The Dutch architect was a wine enthusiast, maybe a connoisseur too. One time, with evident pleasure, he said to me 'the

Beaujolais Nouveau has arrived',[47] and he took me off to one of the city's well-reputed drinking houses! I remember the contentment he showed in tasting the newly made and bottled wine, and in sharing it with me.

The only record we have of Jesus sharing *new wine* with others is in John 2:1-11. Readers will recall the account of the wedding at Cana, in the province of Galilee, to which Mary, Jesus and his disciples were all invited. The festivities were still in full swing when a major hiccup came to the attention of Mary, and probably several other persons; there was no more wine! The text explains how Jesus saved the day by changing water into wine which was served first to the master of the banquet, and then, presumably, to everyone else. The master was impressed by the wine's quality, and considered it to be greatly superior to that which had been served to him earlier in the celebrations. Maybe he esteemed it to be a full-bodied, vintage, mature wine, but in fact it was a very new wine. This miracle, as an illustration of gospel truths, can certainly be understood in more ways than one, but in keeping with our theme I suggest that the six stone (earthenware) jars are symbolic of humankind, more specifically, redeemed and cleansed persons; some interpreters of Scripture numbers tell us that in the number six is the number of man; in their second letter to the Corinthians, Paul and Timothy liken the Christian to a jar of clay, 4:7, 'But we have this treasure in jars of clay to show that this all-surpassing power is from God and not from us.'

---

47. The Beaujolais Region in France is just north of the Massif Central. The wine is a *primeur*, which means it can be sold and consumed as soon as the grape juice has become wine. For some grapes this is particularly early. It has a short fermentation period and can traditionally be purchased from the third Thursday in November.

- The treasure being the light of 'the knowledge of God's glory displayed in the face of Christ' (2 Corinthians 4:6). Such jars are fragile but potentially very useful.

- Water is here a metaphor for God's Word, Scripture (see Ephesians 5:26), which is readily available to all, especially believers, and with which we are encouraged to be filled.

- Water is excellent, but when Jesus fills a believer with the Holy Spirit, the word takes on an added quality, and becomes just like new wine.

- Just as the transformation gave the wedding festivities a noticeable uplift, and greater all-round satisfaction, so the Church militant's impact and capacity to bring joy and gladness into every imaginable situation is wonderfully enhanced when the new wine of the Spirit is freely flowing.

Jesus' teaching on the practice of pouring new wine into new wineskins is very intriguing; each of the synoptic Gospels records what the Master said. Matthew's account, chapter 9:17, reads 'Neither do people pour new wine into old wineskins. If they do, the skins will burst; the wine will run out and the wineskins will be ruined. No, they pour new wine into new wineskins, and both are preserved.' It is commonly understood that the skins were from goats which, with age, became rigid, less flexible and less able to resist the pressure and stress occasioned by a still fermenting young wine. To avoid the risk of an old skin splitting, with the resultant loss of both wine and skin, good practice required that new wine be poured into new wineskins. It is not difficult to discern, in what Jesus said, a metaphor for the work of grace that God effects in all who come to him in repentance and faith; by his Son, Jesus, and by the Holy Spirit, he regenerates (giving new birth and a new nature) and pours his Spirit into the newly created being. 2 Corinthians 5:17 says 'If anyone is in Christ, the new creation has come: the old has gone, the new is here!' The new creature's 'skin' is in the form of a temple, and the 'new wine' in the temple is the Holy Spirit. 'Don't you know that you yourselves are God's temple and that God's Spirit lives among you? . . . God's temple is sacred, and you together are that temple' (1 Corinthians 3:16-17). 1 Corinthians 6:19, in the context of the exhortation in verse 18: 'Flee from sexual immorality', asks a similar question 'Do you not know that your bodies are temples of the Holy Spirit, who is in you, whom you have received from God? You are not your own . . .' The primary application of these texts must certainly be made on a personal basis, but there is surely room for a local community-wide application, and indeed an application to the universal contemporary body of Christ militant is no doubt constantly in view in the divine councils.

Psalm 104:15 reminds us that, in his kindness, God gives 'wine that gladdens human hearts'. This is a reality that many appreciate, but it is also a reality that others voluntarily decline! But why? The reasons are various; however, through the centuries a substantial number of persons have taken a Nazarite vow, or a similar promise, of separation to the Lord, with a commitment to 'abstain from wine and other fermented drink' (Numbers 6:1-4). Samson, Samuel and John the Baptist were all Nazarites; in John's case, the initial commitment was made by his parents prior to his birth, their having received a promise that, as a consequence, their son would be filled with the Holy Spirit even from birth.

It is highly likely that, as it was in Bible days, so it has been ever since: Christians under the influence of a powerful anointing of the Holy Spirit have been assumed, by bystanders, to be under the influence of alcohol. On the Day of Pentecost, all those who were filled with the Holy Spirit spoke in other tongues, in languages they had never learned; many who heard were amazed and asked sensible questions; others mocked the believers, 'made fun of them', saying, 'They have had too much wine' (Acts 2:13). A very lucid Peter, not at all inebriated, spoke clarity into the situation, saying ,'These men are not drunk, as you suppose. It's only nine in the morning!' (v. 15). What followed totally substantiated Peter's stand. There may be some superficial similarity between having drunk too much wine and being filled with the Spirit, but the consequences are diametrically opposed. 'The kingdom of God is not a matter of eating and drinking, but of righteousness, peace and *joy* in the Holy Spirit' (Romans 14:17, my emphasis). This joy knows no hangovers.

As a general rule, a good wine is an expensive wine, but our gracious God offers his best wine for free, along with many other delights and necessities. The Lord declared through Isaiah: 'Come, all you who are thirsty, come to the waters; and you who have no money, come, buy and eat! Come, buy *wine* and milk without money and without cost' (Isaiah 55:1, my emphasis). We do realise, of course, that grace is not cheap; being a disciple of Jesus, appreciating his grace more and more, costs a person everything they have. We are indebted to Dietrich Bonhoeffer for helping us to understand this.[48] God graciously gives the new wine of the Spirit to his children at no cost to them; they are so glad to be so blessed, and the joy of the Lord fills their beings (their new wineskins); nevertheless, sooner or later they learn the lessons of discipleship . . . the price to be paid for following Jesus, the cross to be carried, their bodies (their old skins) to be offered as living sacrifices; for the fullness of the Spirit to remain, a Christian needs to be constantly renewed in body, soul and spirit, and be willing to face the cost of discipleship.

They've run out of wine!

Or as the NIV has it in John 2:3, 'When the wine was gone, Jesus' mother said to him, "They have no more wine."' Several centuries earlier, Israel was in similar straits. In graphic terms, the prophet Joel describes the situation. Drought and locusts had laid waste the territory, and in parallel the moral and spiritual state of the nation had declined to a very low level. Both factually and figuratively, the situation was desperate; no grain, no wine, no oil; through his prophet God calls on the people to rend their hearts and return to him, promising restoration if they obeyed (Joel 2:12-13). They were undeserving of God's bounty, as we are, but when they, and we, repent and return to him, Israel's Lord, and ours, says, 'I am sending you grain, *new wine* and olive oil, *enough to satisfy you fully*' (Joel 2:19, my emphasis), 'the vats will *overflow* with *new wine* and oil' (Joel 2:24, my emphasis). What delightful echoes we have here of New Testament passages concerning the fullness of the Spirit, for example Acts 2:4,

---

48.   Dietrich Bonhoeffer, *The Cost of Discipleship* (London: SCM Press, 2015).

4:8, 6:5, 9:17 and Ephesians 5:18: 'Do not get drunk on wine, which leads to debauchery. Instead, be filled with the Spirit.' The passages cited from Joel relate to Israel's historic situation, and the Church's too. We are called to apply them to the here and now of our pilgrimage in the Church period. In the third chapter of Joel, a future period seems to be in view, a period related to the Day of the Lord: 'In that day the mountains will drip *new wine*, and the hills will flow with milk; all the ravines of Judah will run with water. . . .' (Joel 3:18, my emphasis). In that day there will be no let or hindrance to the plenitude of the Holy Spirit which the Church of Jesus will enjoy. But, as we are all well aware, we are not yet there. We are in the time of intense spiritual combat which precedes the final outpouring of the Spirit. Consequently, Joel's message is also for us.

Our social lives

Our brief look at the subject of new wine as a metaphor for the Holy Spirit began by taking note of Jesus' social life, which was so rich and varied because he lived under a permanent anointing of the Spirit. This is a guide for us, disciples of Jesus, the Christ (the Anointed One), to anoint us with the same Spirit and to do all that is necessary to go about our socialising for his glory.

7

Seal

Folk who communicate the gospel to others are very varied in personality and style: a few are eloquent, persuasive preachers or teachers, able to move crowds, at ease in public; others are of a quieter disposition, happiest when with individuals or small groups, gradually developing friendly and confidence-based relationships, and taking time to introduce their testimony concerning Jesus; then there is the fleeting visitor who straight away conveys the urgency of the message he or she bears, then, unable to stay long because of other even more urgent calls on their time and energy, leaves hurriedly, promising to return 'if it is God's will'.

There were people in Ephesus who came, successively, to know a number of good news bearers, each different in style, all of whom contributed to the gathering in of a harvest of converts for their Lord (the story is related in Acts chapters 18 and 19). First came Paul, accompanied by fellow itinerant missionaries; he stayed a very short time, then left to attend to more urgent business elsewhere, leaving behind an enchanting married couple, Priscilla and Aquila. The couple may not have been noticed by many Ephesians, but they greatly helped another travelling Christian teacher, Apollos, who came to Ephesus after Paul's departure. Apollos was an eloquent, fervent and learned man, well versed in the Scriptures (which at the time meant the Old Testament), and able to teach accurately about Jesus, but his understanding of certain aspects of Christian doctrine was deficient; specifically, the only baptism he knew of was that taught by John the Baptist, a baptism of repentance, and he seemed not to have known much of the Holy Spirit and his workings. Happily, he met up with Priscilla and Aquila, accepted their offer of hospitality, and listened attentively and receptively to their explaining to him 'the way of God more adequately' (18:26). It seems that soon after this, with the encouragement of the brethren, Apollos moved on to Corinth in Achaia where he was a source of great blessing to the Christian community.

But God had more blessing in store for the young community of believers in Ephesus too, for Paul returned, and, finding 'some disciples . . . [he] asked them "Did you receive the Holy Spirit when you believed?" They answered, "No, we have not even heard that there is a Holy Spirit"' (19:1-2). These disciples had believed on Jesus, probably through the ministry of Apollos. Jesus had become their Lord and Saviour, but they were not conscious of the fact that it was the Holy Spirit who had given them salvation and new birth in Christ. After their conversion, they had received water baptism in the doctrinal context taught by John. Hearing this, Paul was enabled to rectify the inadequacy of the teaching they had hitherto received, and they were then baptised into (or in) the name of Jesus.

Certainly, the Holy Spirit was in all that had transpired thus far, but more was to come! Acts 19:6 says 'When Paul placed his hands on them, the Holy Spirit came on them, and they spoke in tongues and prophesied.' These Ephesians who had believed on Jesus and his redemptive work had repented, had been regenerated by the Holy Spirit (although they were unaware that it was the Holy Spirit who had accomplished this wonder), were now baptised in the Holy Spirit. It is, of course, Jesus who baptises in the Spirit; Paul was the Lord's privileged helper.

Some five to seven years after his first visit to Ephesus,[49] Paul wrote to the Christians there from the Roman prison in which he was held. He shared many wonderful truths with them, and for our present purpose we concentrate on one of these; it is spelt out in the first chapter of the letter, verses 13-14; 'And you also were included in Christ when you heard the word of truth, the gospel of your salvation. When you believed, you were *marked in him with a seal, the promised Holy Spirit,* who is a deposit guaranteeing our inheritance until the redemption of those who are God's possession – to the praise of his glory' (my emphasis). Marked with a seal! Paul's readers would have had no difficulty understanding what he meant. In their day, seals of diverse kind were in common use, and they served a number of functions.

Cassel's Book of Knowledge, a children's book, informs its young readers that:

Gem cutting and engraving – the lapidary's art – has been practised from very remote times. Great numbers of precious and semi-precious stones have

---

49.   NIV Study Bible, p. 1631.

been found in Mesopotamia cut into cylindrical form and bearing engraved figures. When rolled over the soft clay of a writing tablet these cylinders left the design in relief to serve as a personal seal. This art had been developed to a high degree of perfection by the ancient Sumerians at least as early as 3,000 B.C. Seals engraved with the sacred beetle, called scarabs, were in use in Egypt by the same time.[50]

A seal is used to identify a paper document as authentic, so to confirm its content, by embossing it. When the word is used figuratively, it refers to something being confirmed or guaranteed.

Common knowledge tells us that a seal can be used as a mark of authority and authenticity on letters etc. to ratify a covenant, to protect books and other documents, to furnish proof, or to secure doors. A seal can be the property of an individual, a family, a nation, a guild or corporation, a business, or much else, and it may, for example, be in the form of an engraved metal cylinder, a signet ring, a stamp or a piece of hardened wax., There was a time when the knots of the string used to secure parcels sent by post were fixed by drops of hot, red molten wax which hardened to form a seal; only the parcel's recipient had the right to break open the seals.

The use of seals is closely linked to such notions as ownership, authenticity and security. It would seem reasonable to assume that these notions were burning in the hearts and minds of the Ephesian Christians when they read 'you were marked . . . with a seal, the promised Holy Spirit' (Ephesians 1:13).

---

50. *Cassel's Book of Knowledge* (ed. Harold F.B. Wheeler; London: The Waverley Book Company, 1930). Volume 4, p. 1547.

The seal of ownership

In the thirty-second chapter of Jeremiah, we learn of how the prophet came to purchase a field from his cousin Hanamel. The transaction was achieved by means of a deed of purchase, of which there were two copies, one of which was signed by both parties, and their witnesses, and sealed; the other was not sealed. Both copies were placed in a clay jar for safe storage. Afterwards, according to custom, the unsealed copy would have been consulted as and when necessary by the parties or their heirs; in the event of doubt or disagreement concerning the content, the seal on the sealed copy would be broken and the authenticity of the unsealed copy determined, or otherwise. In this way, probably also by other, but similar, methods, proof of ownership was determined.

Believers are in the ownership of the Lord God of heaven and earth. A transaction has taken place, been documented, signed and sealed. We are not our own; we have been redeemed by the blood of Jesus; our names are written on his hands and in the Lamb's book of life; the deed has been signed and sealed; we are his. As Paul explained to the Ephesians, the seal of the Spirit is a guarantee, a proof, 'a deposit', a downpayment, so that having 'believed' we have become 'God's possession', awaiting entry into 'our inheritance'. Paul wrote in the same vein to the Christians at Corinth (2 Corinthians 1v22), 'He [God] anointed us, set his seal of ownership on us, and put his Spirit in our hearts as a deposit, guaranteeing what is to come.'

The sense of belonging is quite wonderful, and very essential to we humans as one of the basic elements for full, balanced, happy and fulfilled living; in childhood, it may have been belonging in a group of friends who stuck together through thick and thin; later, it may have been a sports team or some other club, our family, or our church.

But for the Christian the reality of belonging to God, to Jesus, surpasses all other associations and relationships. This profound awareness of belonging infuses the believer with such assurance, such peace, such sense of purpose, such security, such fear of disappointing our owner, and such love, all of which is beyond our ability to comprehend or explain. Maybe that was how the Ephesian Christians felt when they read, and thought about, what the letter they had received said about their belonging to God.

We are not our own, and it behoves us to allow Scripture, and the Spirit, to frequently remind us of this. In his first letter to the Corinthian Christians, Paul was inspired along these lines; having exhorted them very forcefully to 'Flee from sexual immorality', he continues with: 'Do you not know that your bodies are temples of the Holy Spirit, who is in you, whom you have received from God? You are not your own; you were bought at a price. Therefore, honour God with your bodies' (1 Corinthians 6:18-20). No half measures here, and the connection between the seal of the Spirit and the Spirit's indwelling of the believer is clearly implied. Many have sung with conviction these lines by D.W. Whittle:

Not my own, but saved by Jesus,
Who redeemed me by his blood;
Gladly I accept the message,
I belong to Christ the Lord.

Not my own, not my own,
Saviour, I belong to thee!
All I have and all I hope for
Thine for all eternity.[51]

---

51. D.W. Whittle, 'Not My Own', https://hymnary.org/text/not_my_own_but_saved_by_ jesus (accessed 10.8.23). Whittle wrote under the pseudonym El Nathan.

The Holy Spirit stamps a seal of ownership on the redeemed. Malachi 3:17 assures us of the Lord's purpose for his own: '"They will be mine," says the LORD Almighty, "In the day when I make up my treasured possession"' (NIV 1984). Believers are God's possession, and that must be the most important possession truth spelt out in Ephesians 1:3-14; a consequential possession truth is also clearly set forth; it is that those who are in God's ownership are themselves in possession of a magnificent inheritance. The seal of the Holy Spirit attests to this awesome reality; we are owners, with and in Christ, of a glorious inheritance in the heavenly estates and the ages to come.

The seal of authenticity

Maybe you possess documents or objects which bear a seal that demonstrates to everyone that they are authentic. Legal documents such as deeds of sale, diplomas awarded for having successfully passed a college examination, acts of parliament, and lots more, may require the application of a seal in order to be binding in law and considered to be authentic in the eyes of the public concerned.

The paper on which a transaction is written may be very ordinary, but when the deed is signed and attested by the stamp of a seal it becomes a document of weighty importance. Our lives may be like that paper, nothing exceptional in our opinion, maybe in the view of others too, but when God enacts the promise described in Hebrews 10:15-17 (quoting from Jeremiah 31:33-34) we realise that, by grace, our status has changed radically:

The Holy Spirit also testifies to us about this [i.e. *about the absolute sufficiency Christ's sacrifice*]. First he says:

'This is the covenant I will make with them after that time, says the Lord. I will put my laws in their hearts, and I will write them on their minds.' Then he adds: 'Their sins and lawless acts I will remember no more.'

No mention of seal here, but when the Spirit writes, the seal is automatically there. The seal attests that the writing on the heart and mind of a repentant sinner is of God and authentic. The sealed deed is part of the New Covenant of grace.

Satan will endeavour to sow seeds of doubt, even denial, in the hearts and minds of believers, but the Holy Spirit, he who seals, will thwart him by saying, as Paul wrote to the Roman Christians:

The Spirit you received does not make you slaves, so that you live in fear again; rather, the Spirit you received brought about your adoption to sonship. And by him we cry, *'Abba,* Father.' The Spirit himself testifies with our spirit that we are God's children.

(Romans 8:15-16)

Throughout the years of Church history, the matter of authenticity has profoundly exercised Christians; the apostle John, writing towards the end of the first century, when he was probably in his eighties or nineties, addressed the importance of discerning between truth and falsehood; between, on the one hand, spiritual activity authentically of God the Holy Spirit and, on the other, that which is generated by antichrist. In his first letter, John says that the criteria for discerning is: 'Every spirit that acknowledges that Jesus Christ has come in the flesh is from God, but every spirit that does not acknowledge Jesus is not from God' (1 John 4:1-6). A capacity to exercise such discernment, founded upon the seal of the Spirit, is within the ambit of everyone born of the Spirit.

Every new birth is unique and different, although enacted on the same identical principles as every other new birth; and all new births are authentic. 'Now it is God who makes both us and you stand firm in Christ. He anointed us, set his seal of ownership on us, and put his Spirit in our hearts as a deposit, guaranteeing what is to come' (2 Corinthians 1:21-22).

The passport seal

In the contemporary world, most citizens of most countries can obtain a passport which is issued to them by their national government, probably in the name of their head of state. Typically, the passport enables the holder to request entry into another sovereign country, to pass freely, without let or hindrance, and to be afforded such assistance and protection as may be necessary while in a foreign land. Depending on various factors, the request will or will not be granted.

It would seem that the situation regarding the issue of passports in Bible days was rather different, although their function was in most respects the same. In general terms, the issue was not to someone who had requested a passport, but to a person who had been chosen to be a messenger or an emissary of, for example, a corporation, body, country or head of state, to an external authority. Should the head of state be the Roman emperor, his emissary would carry a passport seal bearing an indelible image of the sovereign. Thereby equipped, the travelling representative of the empire would hope for a favourable reception when reaching the frontiers of foreign states!

It is surely not too far-fetched to suggest that the seal of the Spirit, on and within the Christian, is the only passport they have for a lifelong pilgrim journey of service as the Master's representative. A Christian's natural qualities and endowments can, if sanctified, be very helpful in that service, particularly in encounters with fellow human beings, but there are limits beyond which natural talent cannot take us. Journeying with and serving Christ necessitates holding a spiritual passport seal and knowing how to use it.

Here are a few thoughts concerning a Christian's dependence on holding a valid passport; that is the seal of the Holy Spirit (the passport seal):

- It is a vital part of the proof of our right to one day enter heaven, the other essential element being the blood of Christ (Hebrews 10:19); 2 Corinthians 5:5 says: 'Now it is God who has made us for this very purpose [to be with him in heaven] and has given us the Spirit as a deposit, guaranteeing [sealing] what is to come' (NIV 1984). It is confirmation that at his new birth the Spirit placed him in the body of Christ, the Church; 1 Corinthians 12:13 says: '... we were all baptised *by one Spirit* into one body' (NIV 1984, my emphasis); the passport seal of the Spirit assures access to 'Beulah' (married) land (Isaiah 62:4); the Church being the bride of Christ.

- When Christians shows the passport seal to demons and the powers of darkness, they gain access to territory under Satan's control where, in the name of Jesus, they cast out the evil powers;

- In all of our relationships we will, by our conduct and conversation, show the passport seal which, if the image it bears of the Lord of lords is to some degree recognised, will afford some measure of access to the interlocutor's life (the field where gospel seeds can be sown); however, when the passport seal, although clearly presented, is not accepted, the Lord's emissary must leave, praying that a future ambassador will be better received and thus gain access to the territory currently closed; Christians cannot force their way into people's lives; their only authority for seeking entry into the lives of others as an emissary of the kingdom of light is the passport they have received; a passport embossed by the Holy Spirit with a seal, the image of Jesus.

In this connection, much can be learned from the instructions Jesus gave to seventy-two of his followers – those he sent on ahead of him as forerunner-emissaries (Luke 10:1-20). Continuing along the lines of our present imagery, we note that Jesus added two passwords to their 'passports' which they were to use on first contact with persons they met; when entering a home they were to say 'Peace to this house' (v. 5), thus creating a platform of goodwill; and, when entering a town, and being welcomed, they were to heal the sick and say, 'The kingdom of God has come near to you' (v. 9). Most Christians today probably feel that other words and greetings are more appropriate for encounters within their culture and situation! Nevertheless, it is obvious that the principles on which Jesus based his recommendations remain valid today, wherever we are. Whenever the people of the places visited were unwelcoming, the forerunners were to move on, having first warned the unwelcoming that their attitude placed them in danger.

Passport seals are gladly recognised and accepted by fellow Christians, who are happy to welcome the holders into their lives and their communities. In some circumstances, 'letters of recommendation' are useful, and reassuring, for all concerned (2 Corinthians 3:1). But it is better by far to live in the spirit of verses 2 and 3:

> You yourselves are our letter, written on our hearts, known and read by everyone. You show that you are a letter from Christ, the result of our ministry, written not with ink but with the Spirit of the living God, not on tablets of stone but on tablets of human hearts.

May I suggest a very worthwhile, and heart-warming exercise; take fifteen minutes or so to call to memory first encounters with believers you had not previously met, and how each of you instantly recognised the imprint of Christ, the passport seal, on the others' lives. For such rich and happy occasions, we bless the Holy Spirit, he who did the imprinting, the sealing.

The security seal

We noted earlier that parcels, letters too, were once made secure by the application of seals; the same is true of other objects. At the instigation of the Jewish authorities Pilate, the Roman governor, had the tomb, in which Jesus' body lay, made secure; the soldiers 'went and made the tomb secure by putting a seal on the stone and posting a guard' (Matthew 27:66). Jesus who, not long before, had declared that he is the 'resurrection and the life' (John 11:25) didn't need the stone to be removed in order to vacate the tomb; he rose from the dead and simply came out of the sepulchre. But, in order that the disciples could see that Jesus was no longer in the tomb, the seal was broken and the stone displaced, presumably by the angel, or angels. This demonstrated that man-made seals can have their limits! They are not always 100 per cent trustworthy!

The seal of the Holy Spirit on a believer's person is absolutely trustworthy; God will not break it; Satan and his agents do not possess the capacity to break it; the same goes for people, whoever they may be; they, with one possible exception, are powerless to break God's seal. The seal carries the guarantee of Almighty God.

The one possible exception, according to certain passages of Scripture, is the person that the Holy Spirit has sealed, i.e. you and I. Christians are divided in their convictions on this important issue, and we confess to uncertainty on the matter, which is why we use the phrase 'possible exception'.

Those who believe that once saved a person is for always saved, major on John 10:27-29, where we hear Jesus saying of his 'sheep', 'no one will snatch them out of my hand' nor 'out of my Father's hand'.

Those who believe that it is possible to lose one's salvation, while acclaiming the assurance of John 10, consider that the 'no one' does not include the sheep (the person) in the Shepherd's hand; each person always has the right to remove herself/ himself voluntarily from the Shepherd's hand.

Both groups cite Bible passages to explain their position ... but I refrain from commenting further, for that would be beyond this book's scope.

I wish to conclude this section with the resounding doxology at the end of Jude's letter:

To him [Father, Son and Holy Spirit] who is able to keep you from stumbling and to present you before his glorious presence without fault and with great joy— to the only God our Saviour be glory, majesty, power and authority, through Jesus Christ our Lord, before all ages, now and evermore! Amen.

Undoubtedly, the security seal of the Spirit is of incalculable importance in the fulfilment of Jude's confident confession of faith and expectation. By the power and presence of the Spirit, believers are kept from falling and will be presented to God on the Day of the Lord.

When and how is the seal of the Holy Spirit applied?

This is a matter that I would have preferred not to feel necessary to address! I would have enjoyed being able to note that it is an issue on which Christians are universally agreed. This idyllic state is not yet present!

The most widely held views are that:

- The seal is applied at conversion, i.e. at the new birth, and is the Holy Spirit's response to the repentant believer's acceptance of Jesus as Saviour and Lord: 'No one can enter the kingdom of God unless they are born of water [metaphor for God's

Word] and the Spirit' (John 3:5). See also Titus 3:5-6. This is my position.

- The seal is applied at water baptism, infant baptism for some, believer's baptism for others, the mention of water in John 3:5 being understood literally not metaphorically.

The marks of Jesus

The penultimate verse of Paul's letter to the Galatians affirms his unreserved identity with his Lord and Master: 'From now on, let no one cause me trouble, for I bear on my body the marks of Jesus' (Galatians 6:17). What did Brother Paul have in mind? Perhaps the scars left by the whippings he had endured, or the stones that had battered his unimpressive frame, or . . . or . . . ? Who knows? What seems certain to us is that the personal mark of Jesus, the seal of the Holy Spirit, was clearly embossed and apparent on his person.

Bibliography

Adam Clarke, *Commentary on Matthew* (Pokeno, NZ: Titus Books, 2013), Kindle Edition.

A. Donald Miller, *A Bridge of Compassion* (London: Mission to Lepers, 1955).

Alexander Cruden, *Cruden's Complete Concordance to the Old and New Testaments* (London: Morgan and Scott, undated); (Peabody, MA: Hendrickson, 1990; new edition).

Brother Lawrence, *The Practice of the Presence of God* (London: Hodder & Stoughton), 1981.

Cassel's Book of Knowledge, Volume 4 (ed. Harold F.B. Wheeler; London: The Waverley Book Company, 1930).

Dietrich Bonhoeffer, *The Cost of Discipleship* (London: SCM Press), 2015.

George Campbell Morgan, *The Gospel According to Matthew* (Eugene, OR: Wipf & Stock Publishers, 2017).

Jamieson, Fausset & Brown, *Commentary Practical and Explanatory on the Whole Bible* (London: Oliphants Ltd, 1961).

Matthew Henry's Commentary on the Whole Bible, Complete and Unabridged in One Volume (Peabody MA: Hendrickson Publishers, 1991).

J.A. McClymont, ed., *The Century Bible, St John* (Edinburgh: T.C. & E.C. Jack, 1910).

Phillip Keller, *A Shepherd Looks at Psalm 23* (Grand Rapids, MI: Zondervan, 2015).

Redemption Hymnal with Tunes (Revised Edition) (London: Assemblies of God Publishing House, 1955).

Roy Hession, *The Calvary Road* (Fort Washington, PA: Christian Literature Crusade, 1950).

NIV Study Bible (London: Hodder & Stoughton, 1987).

Hugh Mitchell (Compiler), *Gospel Quintet Choruses, Book 1* (Gospel Quintet, 1942).

Coming soon . . .

(an outline of the books that will complete this trilogy).

Book two will be about some of the spheres of Holy Spirit works, including new birth and baptism by the Spirit, baptism in the Holy Spirit, prayer and worship, circumcision of the heart by the Spirit, leading and guiding, the Spirit's gifts and fruit, suffering, the Spirit and the blood of Jesus, and the centrality of Jesus.

Book three will be about the role of the Holy Spirit in association with historical events, including creation, the incarnation, the earthly ministry of the Son, his resurrection, the day of Pentecost, throughout the Church period, in the present world order, and the return to earth of the Son.